STEICHEN
A LIFE IN PHOTOGRAPHY

July 5, 1985

Dear Joe (with apologies to Ogden Nash),
Time is timelessness for you;
Calendars for the human;
What's a year, or thirty, to
Loveliness made woman?

Oh, Night will not see forty-three, again.
Yet soft her wing, Joe;
Pick up your glass and tell me, then—
How old is Spring, Joe?

Love to you and Happy 44th!
Maxine

STEICHEN
A LIFE IN PHOTOGRAPHY

BY EDWARD STEICHEN

Harmony Books / New York

Published in collaboration with The Museum of Modern Art

Acknowledgments

In the preparation of this book I am grateful to the staff of The Museum of Modern Art for their assistance, and in particular to Miss Grace M. Mayer, Curator of The Department of Photography, for her untiring help in many phases of the work. I also want to express my gratitude to Miss Kathleen Haven for her painstaking work in the design of this book.

I owe a very special acknowledgment to my wife, Joanna, who participated with me in preparing the material and encouraged me at every step.

The photographs reproduced in color and duotone in the original edition of this book appear as black-and-white reproductions in the present lower-priced edition.

Published by Harmony Books, a division of Crown Publishers, Inc., One Park Avenue, New York, New York 10016 and simultaneously in Canada by General Publishing Company Limited by arrangement with Doubleday & Company, Inc.

HARMONY and colophon are trademarks of Crown Publishers, Inc.

Designed by Kathleen Haven
Manufactured in Japan
Produced by Chanticleer Press, Inc., New York

Library of Congress Cataloging in Publication Data

Steichen, Edward, 1879–1973.
  Steichen: A life in photography.

  Reprint. Originally published: Garden City, N.Y. : Doubleday, 1963.
  1. Photography, Artistic. I. Title.
TR654.S718 1985   779'.092'4   84-23481
ISBN 0-517-55696-0 (pbk.)

10 9 8 7 6 5 4 3 2 1
First 1985 Harmony Edition

Contents

STEICHEN
A LIFE IN PHOTOGRAPHY

To my mother, Marie Kemp Steichen, 1854–1933,

with homage, gratitude, respect, admiration, and love

The guiding and inspiring influence in my life, she was always an encouraging and a positive force. From my early childhood, she sought to imbue me with her own great strength and fortitude, her deep, warm optimism and human understanding.

As far back as I can remember, she was her family's decision maker. She was married to my father, Jean-Pierre Steichen, in 1876 in the Grand Duchy of Luxembourg. They both came from peasant families. When I was born three years later, she decided that her boy would grow up in America, which she had heard of and dreamt about as the land of freedom, equality, and unlimited opportunity.

When work in the copper mines of Hancock, Michigan, broke my father's health, my mother assumed the responsibilities of breadwinner and opened a millinery shop. In spite of long, tireless hours in her business, she always made time for heart-to-heart conferences with her children. Once, when I was about ten years old, I came home from school, and as I was entering the door of her millinery shop, I turned back and shouted into the street, "You dirty little kike!"

My mother called me over to the counter where she was serving customers and asked me what it was that I had called out. With innocent frankness, I repeated the insulting remark. She requested the customers to excuse her, locked the door of the shop, and took me upstairs to our apartment. There, she talked to me quietly and earnestly for a long, long time, explaining that all people were alike regardless of race, creed, or color. She talked about the evils of bigotry and intolerance. This was possibly the most important single moment in my growth towards manhood, and it was certainly on that day the seed was sown that, sixty-six years later, grew into an exhibition called "The Family of Man."

2 My Little Sister. Milwaukee. 1895. Solio print.

It was during the year 1895, when I was sixteen, that I became interested in owning a camera and in making photographs. A kind, friendly photographic dealer devoted a good deal of time to explaining to me the merits of this or that camera. I bothered him regularly and often, and he showed me every camera in his shop. On one of my visits, he trotted out a smallish, second-hand box camera, which he said was just the thing for me and cheap, too. When he referred to it as a "detective camera," my mind was made up. It certainly was small compared to the other cameras in his shop; compared to the miniature cameras of today, however, it was anything but small.

My mother gave me the money to buy the camera. The Eastman Kodak Company, the makers, said of these cameras, "You press the button, we do the rest." The dealer took the camera into a darkroom and loaded it with a roll of film. This was long before daylight loading film was available. I believe the roll contained fifty exposures. This was an appalling thing in itself, because it meant that I would not see what I was doing until I had made fifty pictures. The dealer explained about exposures, and when I felt I understood this, I went to work.

My first exposure was of our cat sleeping in the show window of my mother's millinery shop. I used up the rest of the roll on various subjects about the house and took the camera back to him. He removed the roll of film and sent it out for developing and printing.

When the film came back, I had a real shock. Only one picture in the lot had been considered clear enough to print. "Clear" was the term of approval given to photographs in those days. And "clear" meant that you could see everything that had been photographed. That one good, or clear, picture was the picture of my little sister playing the piano (plate 2). All the rest were either under- or over-exposed. My father thought one picture out of fifty was a hopeless proposition, but my mother said the picture was so beautiful and so wonderful that it was worth the forty-nine failures.

I don't remember ever having made another roll with the detective camera, for about this time I developed an idea for a practical use for photography. It was during my apprenticeship as a designer in a lithographic firm in Milwaukee. The firm had the highfalutin name of The Ameri-

can Fine Art Company. The apprenticeship there was in the good old German tradition: a four-year term. The first year I was to work for nothing, the second year receive two dollars a week, the third year three dollars a week, and the fourth year four dollars a week. When we designed posters or show cards, we referred to a library of old German magazines and books illustrated by woodcuts which we used as models for copying. The firm did a good deal of work for brewers, flour mills, and pork packers. Neither the pigs nor the wheat shown in our library of old woodcuts looked anything like those I had seen at the Wisconsin State Fair, or during my summer vacations in the country. So I suggested to the manager of the design department that we make photographs. I told him about the pigs I had seen at the state fair and how they differed from the pigs we were making for our pork-packer customers.

"Well," he said, "if you buy a camera, we will give you time off to go and make the pictures you are talking about."

My mother agreed to back me in this idea, so I took the detective camera back to the dealer and explained the situation. Again he showed me all the various cameras, and I settled on a 4 × 5″ camera called a Primo Folding View Camera. It used plates, and I could handle a single photograph at a time and learn how to develop and print the photographs myself. This saved time and was less expensive.

The first thing to do was to set up a darkroom. I found the right kind of room in the cellar, but my mother insisted on removing from it all the preserves she had put up. She didn't like the idea of the processing materials, which she referred to as dangerous, poisonous chemicals, being in the same room with the food. This done, I cut a hole in a partition and covered it with several sheets of what was called post-office paper, a brilliant orange-red material. Outside, on a shelf, I placed a candle. This was my darkroom light. Shielded behind the post-office paper, which was sufficiently inactinic, I could safely watch the entire process of development.

My only reliable information about developing came from the printed instructions in the box of plates. A few moments after I had put the first plate in the tray of developer and begun to rock it vigorously, the image commenced to appear. And when I could identify it as the building I had photographed, I let out a terrific war whoop. My mother came rushing downstairs and called through the door to me, "Is everything all right?"

I said, "You bet it's all right." She thought I had been poisoned and was in agony.

I kept on developing and developing that plate, because I wanted to be sure that I brought everything out. (I had followed the same logic in making the exposure. I had been told that, in sunlight, with the lens stopped down a little, I should give an exposure of one second. But that was the longest one-second exposure that anybody ever gave, for I just kept holding the shutter open longer and longer.) After a little while in the developing tray, the plate became all black and the image disappeared. However, after fixing, if the negative was held up to a strong light, the image could be seen again. I had my Milwaukee skyscraper. Then I took the plate out to the kitchen sink and washed it and washed it. The instructions were to wash for one hour in running water or in sixteen changes of water. I must have washed that plate for two or three hours. I wanted to be sure the washing was thorough.

When the negative was dry the following day, I tried to make prints. But the negative was so dense that it took hours in direct sunlight to get a good image on the solio paper. "Overexposed and overdeveloped," was the verdict of my friend, the dealer, when I showed him the negative and proof.

I now started to make a series of the pictures that we might use as models in the designing department. I made trips into the country during the summer and photographed wheatfields and individual ears of wheat. I found a farmer who grew hops, and I photographed the growing tendrils of hop vines. My crowning achievement was to make some portraits of pigs that were much admired by the pork packers. They insisted that all future placards, posters, and advertising matter be based on the pigs in these photographs.

So my first real effort in photography was to make photographs that were useful. And, as I look back over the many intervening years, I find that usefulness has always been attractive in the art of photography.

Gradually, an interest in photographing things that had

more personal appeal began to take over. Occasionally, I pressed my friends into service for portraiture or for the phantasy pictures that I tried to make, but it was chiefly landscapes, the woods at twilight and dusk, that appealed to me at first.

Usually I developed my negatives at night, and the next day took them to the lithograph shop. During the lunch hour I put the printing frame out on the window sill until the print was the proper depth for toning, which I did at home, at night.

Opportunities for learning about photography were nonexistent in Milwaukee in those days. I knew of no books on the technique of photography. I found a few photographic magazines at the public library, one published in Boston and one in Chicago, but the pictures they reproduced, from professional to amateur photographs, had an air of banality. The library did have books about art and artists, however, and these were really exciting to me. The only art magazine I saw reproduced pictures in color occasionally, but these were rather garish and chromo-like. I particularly remember a color lithograph of an old man playing a violin. It was made from a painting by J. G. Brown. My mother said this man looked exactly like her brother, and I copied the picture in oil colors as a Christmas present for her, much to her delight and, I may say, pride.

I was also painting in my spare time, and painting presented problems of expression similar to those I encountered in photography. The romantic and mysterious quality of moonlight, the lyric aspect of nature made the strongest appeal to me. Most of the paintings—watercolors—that I did at that time were of moonlight subjects.

Although painting offered unlimited opportunities to deviate from the purely naturalistic, I found that I brought to painting some of the discipline of the literal that was inherent in photography. The moonlight subjects appealed to me on a romantic basis, but I made realistic notes of the actual night colors on the spot, describing the colors I saw in terms of the mixture of pigments to be used in the painting. Today, in retrospect, I believe my work as a photographer had a greater influence on my painting than my work as a painter had on my photography.

In 1896 or 1897 I got together a small group of fellows about my own age. We were all engaged in professions that had to do with pictures. We rented a small room in an office building and hired a model in order to get some experience drawing from life rather than from pictures. We also secured the voluntary services of an old German painter, Richard Lorence, who criticized our work.

Our small coterie started to grow. Within a year working space was donated to us in the basement of the Ethical Culture Society's building, and we gave our group a name, the Milwaukee Art Students' League. I was elected its first president. The League continued to grow and is today a large organization of recognized importance in Milwaukee.

In those early days we often discussed the abilities of contemporary artists. One evening, during the model's rest period, we were having a particularly violent discussion about some academic painter when in walked Richard Lorence. He sat down near the door and smoked his pipe. At the end of the rest period, he got up and in his deep, almost guttural voice said, "Enough of the 'dummheit' [foolishness]. This talk, talk, talk, talk, talk. You are here to learn how to draw by drawing, not by talking. When you can draw me a shoe that looks like a shoe with a foot in it, then you will have a foundation on which to form opinions. Now you have not."

Richard Lorence, whose sometimes oversimplified counsel carried weight which we all absorbed and remembered, was not interested in photography as such. He said I was wasting my time with it. The best he could ever say of a photograph was, "Well, that's a good one. It would make a fine painting."

For many years, that was the usual attitude of painters toward photography. A photograph would suggest something that could be done better in a painting. The end-all and be-all of a photograph was to record. If you could positively identify everything, it was clear and therefore a good photograph. When one tried to go beyond that concept, the only way to learn was by trial and error, and chiefly by error.

The question of clear pictures and sharp pictures became a subject of controversy at the League. To me, the mood and the lyric feeling aroused in relation to the woods seemed more important. Because I found nature most beautiful in twilight and moonlight, all my efforts were directed toward finding a way of interpreting such moments. By taking a streetcar out to the end of the line and walking a short distance, I could find a few wood lots.

These became my stamping grounds, especially during autumn, winter, and early spring. They were particularly appealing on gray or misty days, or very late in the afternoon and at twilight. Under those conditions the woods had moods, and the moods aroused emotional reactions that I tried to render in photographs. I made many experiments, lengthening or shortening the time of exposure, making the prints darker or lighter, changing the time of development. Some experiments led to a better rendering of mood, but several accidents also contributed.

One autumn day, during a heavy overcast, I set up my camera to photograph the bare tree trunks on a large wood lot. While I was working, a few drops of rain fell. Checking the image on the ground glass of the camera, I saw that the whole scene had been transformed by general diffusion. A few raindrops, I found, had accumulated on the face of the lens. When I wiped off the raindrops, the scene on the ground glass became clear again.

On another occasion, while I was making an exposure of several seconds, I accidentally kicked the tripod, causing the camera to vibrate. This action produced an entirely different kind of diffusion in the photograph.

Since diffusion by either action could be reproduced at will, my technical vocabulary took a lurch forward. When prints from plates so produced were shown at the lithographic shop or at the art class, the response was often, "Gee, that's artistic!" "Artistic" seemed to be something to strive for. Getting beyond literal facts was one achievement, at any rate, that was approved of.

There was a landscape painter, famous in Milwaukee, who was particularly applauded for the way he painted trees. At one of his exhibitions a young lady approached him and said, "Oh, Mr. Viandon, you paint such wonderful trees. What is your secret?"

And he said, "Secret? Vat is a tree? A tree is one hundred t'ousand leaves. You paint one hundred t'ousand leaves and dere you have a tree."

During those teen-age years, I knew, of course, that trees and plants had roots, stems, bark, branches, and foliage that reached up toward the light. But I was coming to realize that the real magician was light itself—mysterious and ever-changing light with its accompanying shadows rich and full of mystery. The haunting, elusive quality of twilight excited in me an emotion that I felt compelled to evoke in the images I was making. Emotional reaction to the qualities of places, things, and people became the principal goal in my photography.

By 1898 I was more or less in control of the rendering of those moods and moments. I was an "impressionist" without knowing it. "The Pool—Evening" (plate 8) was, in fact, a picture of just a puddle of water with mud clots protruding. The technical problem was solved by setting the focus on the flat foreground and regulating the resulting diffusion in the woods by opening or closing the diaphragm of the lens. In the dark picture "Woods—Twilight" (plate 9) the diffusion was produced by wetting the lens. The print "Edge of Woods" (plate 11), the most abstract of the group, was produced by setting up a vibration in the camera during exposure.

The question of composition was bandied about freely and often at the Art Students' League, and I began to recognize the role of composition in the expression evoked by any image. At first, I could determine the exact composition only by cropping the print, but, gradually, I learned to compose on the ground glass before making the exposure. This was the case in "The Pool—Evening" and "Woods—Twilight."

During all this time, I did plenty of photography of the usual kind: portraits, friends, mementoes, photographs of groups at the picnics and social outings of the Milwaukee *Turnvereins* and singing societies. There, clearness and definition were most important. These jobs brought in twenty-five or fifty cents a print and paid for other, more serious experimental work.

In the issue of *Harper's Weekly* of November 5, 1898, appeared an article by Charles H. Caffin entitled "The Philadelphia Photographic Salon." Caffin's article described, as an artistic event, an exhibition of photographs held at the Pennsylvania Academy of the Fine Arts. This exhibition was the result of a joint effort by the Photographic Society of Philadelphia and the Pennsylvania Academy of Fine Arts. The stated purpose of the salon was to exhibit "only such pictures produced by photography as may give distinct evidence of individual artistic feeling and execution."

Fifteen hundred photographs had been submitted to the jury, and 259 were selected. The jury was made up of two well-known painters, William M. Chase and Robert Vonnoh; an illustrator, Alice Barber Stevens; and two photographers, Alfred Stieglitz and Robert S. Redfield.

Caffin's article described many of the pictures in appreciative detail. Curiously, he decried photography that imitated painting, but praised "A Woman in White," by Clarence H. White, as being like a Sargent painting. Mrs. Gertrude Käsebier, of New York, was the only exhibitor honored by having as many as ten photographs accepted by the jury. Caffin spoke of her prints in the highest terms and referred to one of her portraits as being like a Whistler. He devoted considerable space to the work of F. Holland Day, whose photographs had been given the place of honor in the exhibition.

This was the first time that photographs had been shown in an art museum in America or, perhaps, anywhere. It was the most stimulating and exciting thing I had heard of in photography. Here was the knowledge that there were serious photographers at work in Europe and America, and that the oldest art institution in America was interested enough to exhibit their photographs.

At the next session of the Art Students' League, I read this article to my fellow students, who were almost as much agog about it as I was. One of the girls piped up, "Why don't you send some of your photographs to the next exhibition?" The response was guffaws and giggles from some of the students, but then and there, I made up my mind that if there ever was another such exhibition, I would submit some of my own photographs.

Later, the photographic magazines also published articles about this exhibition. Their comments, mostly derisive, did not interest me so much as the reproductions of some of the photographs from the exhibition that were also printed. The work of Clarence White made a particular impression on me, although the articles ridiculed the poetic viewpoint in his photography and referred to him as a grocery clerk from Newark, Ohio.

Now that I had ordained myself a would-be exhibitor at the next salon, the problem was what to send, and the first conclusion I came to was one of prudence. It seemed unwise to compete with older, more experienced, and better photographers than I.

I went through all my photographs and selected prints that were unlike any that I saw reproduced or described in the various articles about the exhibition. One selection was a composition study in which I had used myself as a model, and the other was a print that most of my colleagues at the League had praised. It was always referred to as

"Lady in the Doorway" (plate 4), and this is the way it came to be taken.

The mother of one of the students at the League had a beautiful estate, Gordon Place, on the Milwaukee River, and she turned over one of the houses on the estate to the Art Students' League for the summer. For the opening festivities of our summer quarters, we had decorated the house with boughs and branches. Early on the day of our housewarming, I had set up my camera to photograph the sunlight coming in the doorway. Suddenly, one of the girl students appeared in the door, and I asked her to stay there while I made the picture. While setting the camera and checking the image on the ground glass, I had automatically brought the image into sharp focus. After trying it in and out of focus several times, I decided it gave a better feeling of light when it was out of focus than when it was sharp. So I deliberately made the picture out of focus.

Both pictures were made on small, 4 × 5″ plates, and from the descriptions of the pictures in the previous Philadelphia salon it sounded as if they were all much larger. Since I had no equipment for enlarging or any knowledge about the process, I went to see a young man who operated a professional portrait studio and explained my problem to him. He made enlargements for me on Royal Bromide Paper, a rough-textured paper with a creamy tone. And when the time came around, the two enlargements, in simple frames, were sent off to the jury of the Second Philadelphia Photographic Salon.

The prints were accepted and hung by the jury. I never heard of any bells being rung for them, but I did receive a letter from Clarence White, saying that my two pictures showed originality—"a quality which needs to be encouraged."

Soon after came the announcement from Chicago of a salon to be held there early in 1900. I had been very active meanwhile with a new and larger camera and had made many experiments. Enlargements were no longer necessary.

In one of the photographic magazines, I had read an article by Robert Demachy, a famous French photographer, about a process that he used extensively and referred to as a gum-bichromate process. This was a pigment process similar to the well-known carbon process, but he coated the paper himself. It appealed to me for two reasons. One

was economy, and the other was the unusual quality that could be produced, unlike anything printed on silver or platinum paper. The ingredients used in coating the paper were simply watercolor, in black, brown, or almost any other shade, and gum arabic. The sensitizing agent was bichromate of potash. The mixture was applied to paper with a brush as evenly as possible. When dry, it became light sensitive. When it was placed under a negative and exposed to light, the action of the light hardened the pigment under the thin open parts of the negative, making it relatively insoluble. The paper was developed by floating it on cold, warm, or even hot water. Sometimes it took friction with a brush to remove the parts that were affected less by light. If the mixture was applied thick, the results were very granular, an excellent effect for some pictures representing broad masses of light and dark. When a thin coating was applied, it gave finer gradation and less grain. The paper was inexpensive to produce, and gave greater control of the final result than any other process.

I was always intrigued with the possibility of producing by photography a picture as good as one that could be done in any other way, and the gum process gave me a chance to develop this idea along extreme lines. The picture "Polly Horter" (plate 5) was printed on charcoal paper in two printings and was deliberately made to produce an effect similar to that of a charcoal drawing. I also made prints at that time in two different tints.

When the time came to send in prints for the Chicago salon, I took the bull by the horns and submitted the full allotment of ten prints to the jury. Clarence White, who was a member of the Chicago jury, saw my prints as they were unpacked and wrote to me, "Here are ten that will go in as a block." But White was premature in his judgment. When they came up before the jury, all but three were turned down.

In the meantime, for almost a year, I had been making plans for the future.

When my four years' apprenticeship at the lithographic company ended, I started immediately at twenty-five dollars a week, and by 1898 I was making fifty dollars, a great deal of money in those days. When I announced I was going to quit the job and go to Europe, my father thought I was crazy. But my mother, as usual, gave a sympathetic ear. She even promised to add to my own savings so that I could go. In the spring of 1900, a few weeks after my twenty-first birthday, I started off for New York en route to Paris with my friend Carl Björncrantz, a member of the Milwaukee Art Students' League. The sight of New York, impressive enough, became doubly so when I saw an outdoor advertisement that was designed after one of my posters for Cascarets. For the company's theme, "They work while you sleep," I had painted an attractive young woman asleep, with the "C" of "Cascarets" forming her bed. It covered the whole side of a warehouse building six stories high and a block long. I decided then and there that New York must be the art center of the world.

Clarence White had urged me to stop off and see Alfred Stieglitz at the New York Camera Club. Stieglitz, he said, was the leader in the struggle for the recognition of pictorial photography as an art. When I arrived at the Camera Club, Stieglitz was putting up a members' exhibition, and he introduced me to Joseph Keiley, who was assisting him. I had examples of my photographs and paintings with me, and although he was busy, Stieglitz gave me over an hour and expressed warm interest in my plans. He seemed particularly interested in the fact that I was both a painter and a photographer. He bought three of my prints for five dollars apiece, saying, "I am robbing you, at that." But, to me, this was a princely price.

As I left, he went with me to the elevator, and as the door closed, he said, "Well, I suppose now that you're going to Paris, you'll forget about photography and devote yourself entirely to painting."

As the elevator went down, I shouted up to him, "I will always stick to photography!"

3 Self Portrait. Milwaukee. 1898. Platinum print.

4 Lady in the Doorway. Milwaukee. 1897. First photograph exhibited (Philadelphia Salon, 1899).

5 Polly Horter. Milwaukee. 1899. Gum print.

6 My Little Sister with the Rose-covered Hat. Milwaukee. 1899. Platinum print.

7 Self Portrait with Sister. Milwaukee. 1900. Platinum print.

8 *(opposite)* The Pool—Evening. Milwaukee. 1899. Platinum print.

9 *(above)* Woods—Twilight. Milwaukee. 1899. Platinum print.

10 Melting Snow. Milwaukee. 1899. Platinum print.

11 *(below)* Edge of Woods. Milwaukee. 1899. Platinum print.

12 *(next page)* Woods in Rain. Milwaukee. 1899. Platinum print.

After four or five days in New York, Björncrantz and I checked our bicycles on the French Line steamer *Champlain*. We had booked passage by steerage, and steerage in those days was an experience. The sleeping quarters ran the full length of one deck, and the bunks were tiers of three shelves, one above the other, with straw and a blanket for bedding. Food was ladled out from buckets onto tin plates that the passengers had to wash in cold water. Having been warned that the food was poor, we took a number of loaves of bread, a ham, and some cheese with us, and Björncrantz and I lived on these for the seven or eight days that it took to make the trip.

After a day or two in Le Havre, Björncrantz and I got on our bicycles and photographed and sketched our way along the winding curves and bends of the Seine River to Paris. It was a wonderful introduction to France in the spring, with the orchards and meadows in bloom.

One of our fellow passengers on the ship had a sister living in Montmartre, and he had given us her address. The sister, who was the *concierge* of the building, had a spare room in the attic for rent. We took the room, washed up, and made tracks for the Rodin exhibition just outside the gates to the Paris World's Fair of 1900.

In the spring of 1898, the Milwaukee papers had carried stories about a sensational art controversy raging in Paris. It seemed that, seven years before, the sculptor Auguste Rodin had been commissioned by the Society of Men of Letters to make a statue of Balzac for the city of Paris. In the Salon of 1898, Rodin exhibited the plaster cast of the finished statue, and in the opening hours of the exhibition, crowds gathered around the statue, and vehement discussions took place pro and con. When the Society of Men of Letters decided to refuse the statue, the newspapers enjoyed a heyday with the scandal, intensifying the feeling in Paris. The Balzac statue was called a monstrosity by some and by others a sack of flour with a head stuck on top.

When I saw it reproduced in the Milwaukee newspaper, it seemed the most wonderful thing I had ever seen. It was not just a statue of a man; it was the very embodiment of a tribute to genius. It looked like a mountain come to life. It stirred up my interest in going to Paris, where artists of Rodin's stature lived and worked.

Another French artist who had lighted up my imagination was Claude Monet. In the Milwaukee public library I had read an article about him. Here was a landscape painter, it said, who went out and painted landscapes on the scene, instead of painting them from memory in his studio. The article went on to say that Monet let light and air into landscape painting. As I read, it seemed to me that he worked on canvas the way I tried to work with a camera.

Björncrantz and I arrived at the Rodin exhibition late in the afternoon, just before closing hour. The light was dim. In the center of the gallery stood the Balzac, looking positively gigantic. In one corner of the gallery, I saw, talking earnestly to several people, a stocky man with a massive head, almost like a bull's. I felt, instinctively, that this must be the master himself, and I made up my mind I was going to photograph him someday.

A few days later, I went to the Louvre and had an experience for which I was totally unprepared. I made my firsthand acquaintance with the Old Masters. What a fabulous collection of painting and sculpture! Then there was the Luxembourg museum of living artists. That signified modern art, most of it very uninteresting, but one room contained a collection of the Impressionists, whom I had read and dreamed about. Here were Monet and Degas and Manet, Pissarro and Sisley. The Monets stirred me most. They dealt with something that was still well out of the domain of photography, the magic and color of sunlight.

Altogether, the first week in Paris was overwhelming. Everywhere I turned, I found a new experience, a revelation.

In the early autumn, I went to London with the idea of submitting some of my photographs to the exhibitions of the Royal Photographic Society and the Linked Ring. There I met F. Holland Day, one of the important American photographers. He was in London to arrange for an exhibition of what he called the New School of American Photography, and the Royal Photographic Society had turned over their exhibition rooms to him. Now, for the first time, I saw photographs by outstanding photographers. It was an exciting experience.

Day was a Boston publisher who published beautiful

editions of books, along the lines of William Morris. He had some books with him, and they certainly were handsome, but it was his photographs that really excited me. He had a special lens that had been made for him in Boston by the optical firm of Pinkham and Smith. The Smith lens was deliberately uncorrected. Photographs made with it had an effect similar to that of some I had made with a wet lens. The image was quite sharp, but all the light tones had a halo around them. This lens was later adopted by almost all the leading American photographers and by many of the Europeans.

Day selected twenty-one of my prints to be included in this exhibition—and I now was a member of the New School of American Photography!

When the exhibition opened, it was like a bombshell exploding in the photographic world of London. Day's individual exhibit was the largest of any in the group, and he referred to the showing as an exhibition of prints by the New School of American Photography supplemented by an additional collection of one hundred examples of the work of F. Holland Day. But the term that stuck was the New School of American Photography. It was a red rag waving in the face of the public, and the press had a holiday making fun of it.

Compared to the work by the British and European photographers that I saw at the annual Royal Photographic Society Exhibition and the Linked Ring Exhibition, Day's American Exhibition certainly was of a new school. Many of the American photographs were in a very much lower key than any of the work of the European exhibition, and included many fine landscapes.

Day's religious pictures came in for severe criticism. One critic said that it remained for a Yankee from Boston to perpetrate this insult on the British public. Those who said it was not proper to portray religious subjects in so literal a process as photography seemed to forget that, all through the ages, artists had painted religious pictures from living models. I failed to see any legitimate reason why a photographer should not have the same privilege that a painter has in doing religious subjects. The religious series was only a very small part of Day's work, however, and his reputation is not based on them.

Day was an aesthete in everything he did. His manner of mounting and presenting his photographs, using crayons and charcoal and drawing papers in multiple mount-

ings, was certainly of this order, and his photography leaned more to over-refinement than to emotional power.

F. Holland Day was the first man to assemble a collection consisting exclusively of the work of men and women later recognized as leaders in the most important American movement in pictorial photography. Among the pioneers, he was in a class with Alfred Stieglitz.

When I asked Day why he did not show any of Alfred Stieglitz's photographs in this exhibition, he explained that, in spite of much urging, Stieglitz had refused to be a part of it. Day said that Stieglitz was opposed to the exhibition and had tried to stop it. Later, when I got to know Stieglitz and asked him about the incident, he said he had been opposed to Day's exhibition because he did not think it was adequate and because Day had had nothing but second- and third-rate prints by the photographers he was including. I ultimately became closely acquainted with the work of these photographers, and I never saw better prints from their hands than those exhibited by Day. As far as adequate representation is concerned, I do not think that, except for Stieglitz, any photographer whose work was even moderately known at that time was excluded from Day's exhibition, as his catalogue proves. Day disapproved of *Camera Notes,* the magazine Stieglitz was editing at the time for the New York Camera Club. He referred to it as a tasteless publication.

After the fuss and excitement in London, I was ready to get back to Paris and go to work. But before leaving, I made a photograph of the venerable painter George Frederick Watts (plate 13). This was the beginning of the portrait series I had planned to make of distinguished artists in Europe. I hoped to include painters, sculptors, literary men, and musicians.

In Paris, I had found a studio that an American illustrator was vacating, and I now found myself a resident of the Rive Gauche at 83 boulevard du Montparnasse. It was a long, low studio building, and I had a large, well-lighted studio on the second floor.

I enrolled as a student at the Julian Academy. I appeared there on a Monday morning with my portfolio, drawing paper, and charcoal, and took up a position in one of the classrooms. We had a magnificent, tall, Italian athlete for a model. He assumed a grandiose pose of simulated action, legs spread as if climbing, one foot on a box, and a long staff in his hand. For the first time I was going to have a whole week in which to make a drawing, instead of the half-hour periods for sketching that we had had in Milwaukee. I was stirred by the project and the model, and I commenced to sketch in the action of the pose, working slowly and deliberately.

On Wednesday, Jean-Paul Laurens, the instructor, came round to criticize the work. He sat down near me at the place of a young man from Poland. This man had a large sheet of paper braced up on a chair in front of him, but he had been working on a small image, not more than ten inches high, in the middle of the paper. I had looked occasionally from my work to his with surprise. He was more concerned with smoothing out the surfaces than anything else. Jean-Paul asked him whether he was drawing the figure in front of us. The boy nodded his head, and Jean-Paul exploded, "Well, why don't you do it! This soft smooth thing has none of the spirit of the magnificent specimen of a man in front of you. You should fill the paper, sketch in the action and outline of the pose. Get the force and vigor, the bone structure and the anatomy of the model and not this soft nothingness you have on the paper."

As Jean-Paul got up and approached the easel where I was working he turned, grabbed the young man he had been criticizing so harshly, pulled him around, and told him to look at my drawing. He said, "This is the way to do it. See this outline... all the action and vitality has been reproduced. And look at that hand. That's the way Michelangelo drew a hand!"

I had gooseflesh all over. My hair commenced to rise. Everybody in the classroom looked round to see who the new Michelangelo was. After Jean-Paul departed, the young Pole packed up his drawing paper and went home. We never saw him again. I just stood staring at my drawing. It started to swim in front of me, and I was afraid to touch it, afraid I would spoil the miraculous thing I had done. Occasionally, some one of the Frenchmen who had been at the school a long time would come and look casually over my shoulder, grunt, and walk on. By Wednesday, one of these expert pupils had finished a drawing and moved into the young Pole's place to begin a new one. But I went at my drawing in a very gingerly manner. Nothing would have induced me to touch that hand.

When Friday came, Jean-Paul made the rounds for the final criticism. He sat down at the place of my new neighbor, the star student, rubbed his hands, and said, "Very good, very good." He suggested a hairline off the calf of one leg, and then, with a little rubber stamp, he made a purple mark, "JPL," on the drawing. It meant that this was one of the best drawings of the week.

Then he stood up next to me. He looked at my drawing and said, "Are you doing this from that model there?"

I said, "Yes sir."

"Well, why don't you do something with it? Put some modeling into it. Put some texture on it."

He paused for a moment. Then he said, "Look at that. That is not a hand, that is a block of wood!" He looked at that hand just as he had looked at the young Pole's drawing on Wednesday.

Out of a corner of my eye, I saw wry smiles on some of my colleagues' faces. All I could do was take it. I couldn't answer back and complain that he had approved the hand two days before.

The following week, I came back with oil color and canvas and started to paint. On Wednesday, when Jean-Paul entered the classroom, I quietly took my painting off the easel and left the room until he was gone. Then I brought it back and continued working. I did the same on Friday. But I decided to follow the young Polish lad's footsteps and call it quits with the Julian Academy. The kind of work that was admired there was cold, lifeless, slick, smoothly finished academic drawing. I was not interested, and after two weeks at the Julian Academy, my professional art training came to an end.

I took up photography actively again, sometimes painted or photographed a model, and spent a great deal of time in the Louvre. After the first overwhelming impact, I began studying the individual pictures and schools more closely and found myself wondering repeatedly whether such and such a painting could also be done by photography. One Titian particularly intrigued me, "Man with a Glove." It had been painted with great precision, but it also had style and an allure that I found hard to explain.

About this time, F. Holland Day arrived from London with the photographs from the New American School exhibition. He had brought them to Paris with the idea of showing them there. I invited him to share my studio with me, and he seemed pleased to do so.

I painted a portrait of Day and sent it to the Salon National des Beaux-Arts. It was accepted and hung in one of the important galleries.

One day, I dressed up in one of Day's stocks, draped his mantle around my shoulders, picked up a palette and brush, and posed in the mirror for what I thought was going to be photography's answer to "Man with a Glove." I experimented with prints from the negative, first with the original gum-print process, then with other colloids, glues, and gelatins, sometimes in combination, sometimes separately. I worked out several formulas that gave interesting results and considerable leeway in controlling the results. It took me almost a year to master the technique and get the kind of print I wanted (plate 18).

When Day's exhibition opened at the Photo Club of Paris, it was greeted with some degree of the shock that had met the exhibition in London, but with none of the vituperation or wry humor. Robert Demachy, the leading pictorial photographer in France, referred to my work as that of the *"Enfant Terrible"* of the New American School.

The event that made 1901 memorable to me was the opportunity to realize my dream of knowing Auguste Rodin. I had been asked, tentatively, to photograph the two charming children of Fritz Thaulow, a popular Norwegian landscape painter living in Paris. He invited me to lunch at his home, a beautiful house on the boulevard Malesherbes, and with a portfolio of my prints strapped on my bicycle I pedaled across Paris. I showed the prints and received the order to photograph the children. During the luncheon, I mentioned my excitement at seeing the Rodin exhibition and confessed how eager I was to meet the sculptor. Thaulow said, "We know him well. We are friends. Since you have your bicycle, we will all bicycle out to Meudon this afternoon to see him." Meudon is one of the suburbs of Paris.

On the way out, Fritz said to Madame Thaulow, "Now, Rose will probably ask us for dinner, but we will be adamant and refuse to put her to that trouble." Rose was Madame Rodin. I secretly hoped she would be more adamant in her insistence than the Thaulows would be in their refusal.

Rose met us and said that Rodin was still in town but would be out soon, and she made us comfortable in the garden.

Late in the afternoon, there appeared over the brow of the hill a stocky figure walking rapidly towards the house. I recognized Rodin from the brief glimpse I had had at the exposition. There were the usual formal introductions, and then Rodin and Rose both insisted that we stay for dinner. When Rodin insisted, that's all there was to it. We stayed. Japanese paper lanterns were strung up in the trees. Rose set the table and disappeared into the kitchen for a while. Then we sat down to a marvelous dinner, which was accompanied by wines that Rodin brought up from the cellar.

After dinner, with the liqueur and cigars, Fritz said to me, "Now bring out your portfolio." I did so with fear and trembling. Rodin went through the prints slowly, pausing now and then to look at one for some time, and giving grunts of approval and, sometimes, words. When it was all over, I blurted out that the great ambition of my life was to do a portrait of him. He clapped his hand on my shoulder and said to Thaulow, "You see, Fritz, enthusiasm is not dead yet."

He assured me that I could photograph him whenever I desired. I asked if it would be possible to visit him in his studio first in order to make plans for the picture. This pleased him, and he said I could come any time and often, especially on Saturday afternoons, when he usually did not work but received friends and visitors.

And so, practically every Saturday for a whole year, I visited and studied Rodin while he walked among his works. Finally, having decided just what I wanted to do, I made an appointment and went down with my camera. I asked him to stand next to the statue of the "Victor Hugo" and face "Le Penseur." But since the studio was filled to capacity with large blocks of sculptured marble and with plaster, bronze, and clay being worked on, there was not enough room for me to get Rodin, the "Victor Hugo," and "Le Penseur" on one plate. So I made an exposure that included Victor Hugo with Rodin. Then I moved my camera over and photographed "Le Penseur" separately, explaining to Rodin that I was going to join them both in one picture later. In those days, I had only one lens, a rapid rectilinear lens of relatively long focus. If I had had a wide-angle lens, I probably would have made the whole thing in one shot.

I didn't know enough about the technical problems to solve the job of uniting the two pictures at once, and at first I printed only the negative of Rodin standing near Victor Hugo. Later, I worked out a technique by which

I could combine the two negatives and make one print, as it is shown in plate 16.

When I showed Rodin the combined print, he was elated. And Judith Cladel, who later wrote a wonderful biography of Rodin, looked at the photograph, and said to Rodin, "Ah, it is Rodin. It is you between God and the devil." He replied simply, "Mais oui," and laughed heartily. He was quite proud of the picture and showed it to everybody.

During the same session, I had made a number of heads of him that were more like conventional portraits (plates 14 and 15), but the silhouette of that massive head appeals to me as more like the Rodin who created the Balzac than any of the others. It is probably more of a picture *to* Rodin than it is *of* Rodin, because after all, it associates the genius of the man with that expressed by his work. Today, one bronze cast of "Le Penseur" has an honored place in front of the Pantheon in Paris and another looks down on the ground where Rodin and Rose are buried at Meudon.

When my year's lease of the studio on the boulevard Montparnasse was up, I moved to a larger studio in the rue Boissonade. At about that time, a photographer who made a specialty of photographing paintings seen at the salons invited me over to his place to see an exhibition of paintings which he called *"très intéressantes."* There, in a small room, not much more than ten or twelve feet square, the walls were covered from floor to ceiling with paintings hung one right next to the other, unframed. They were unlike any I had ever seen or heard about. It was one of the biggest shocks I had ever had. If this was great painting, then everything that I had conceived and learned was wrong. At the same time, I felt conscious of a curious force and power in these pictures. The contradictory experience was too much for me, and I was actually nauseated. The paintings were by a man named Van Gogh.

I went back again a second day and looked at the Van Goghs more calmly. This time, as on the day before, I was the only visitor. Three pictures of the now celebrated sunflower series made a particular and most dramatic appeal to me. My friend, the photographer, told me that not one painting had been sold. When I asked him how much they were, he said, "A thousand francs will buy one." At present-day prices there were at least two million dollars worth of painting in that room available for $200 each, but with no purchasers, not even visitors.

That year, 1901, I also went to Munich to see the exhibition of the German Secessionist painters. While there, I photographed Franz von Lenbach, the German portrait painter. I photographed him much in the manner in which he had made some of his famous self-portraits. Among these were some that showed him wearing a large, broad-brimmed hat. After I had photographed him with palette and brush, I asked him if I could photograph him wearing his hat. He looked around for the hat and could not find it. Then he grabbed mine, which was also broad-brimmed, and clapped that on his head. The photograph of Lenbach wearing my hat appears in plate 20.

I did a number of nude figures in Paris, some of which are shown on plates 24 through 28. In none of these figures is the face visible. For many years everyone had prejudices against posing in the nude, and even professional models usually insisted, when they posed for nude pictures, that their faces not be shown.

In 1902, shortly before my return to New York, I had a one-man show at the Maison des Artistes on the rue Royale in Paris, which included both paintings and photographs. The photographs were divided into two series. Series A contained straight prints without any manipulation or retouching. Series B consisted of prints obtained by different processes that permitted manipulation in varying degrees. In the exhibition catalogue, I referred to Section B as *Peinture à la Lumière,* Painting with Light.

Among the visitors to this exhibition was Maurice Maeterlinck, whom I had photographed in 1901 (plate 23). His books *Treasure of the Humble* and *Wisdom and Destiny* had had a great influence on me. He was one of the few visitors who took a lively interest in the photographs in my exhibition and studied them very carefully. During his visit, he expressed ideas about photography that were different and more considered than any I had heard before. I told him that many of the pictures were going to be reproduced in *Camera Work,* an important American magazine, and wondered whether he would put down some of his thoughts to be included in the same issue. He said he would be glad to do that.

The article he wrote arrived in New York late, after the magazine had already gone to press. But we were all so impressed with what he had written that Stieglitz arranged to have it included as a special insert. It was printed both in a facsimile of the original French manuscript and in English translation.

Maeterlinck said, in part: "I believe that here are observable the first steps, still somewhat hesitating but already significant, toward an important evolution. Art has held itself aloof from the great movement, which for half a century has engrossed all forms of human activity in profitably exploiting the natural forces that fill heaven and earth. Instead of calling to his aid the enormous forces ever ready to serve the wants of the world, as an assistance in those mechanical and unnecessarily fatiguing portions of his labor, the artist has remained true to processes which are primitive, traditional, narrow, small, egotistical, and overscrupulous, and thus has lost the better part of his time and energy....

"It is already many years since the sun revealed to us its power to portray objects and beings more quickly and more accurately than can pencil or crayon....

"But today it seems that thought has found a fissure through which to penetrate the mystery of this anonymous force, invade it, subjugate it, animate it, and compel it to say such things as have not yet been said in all the realm of chiaroscuro, of grace, of beauty and of truth."

13 George Frederick Watts. London. 1901. Pigment print.

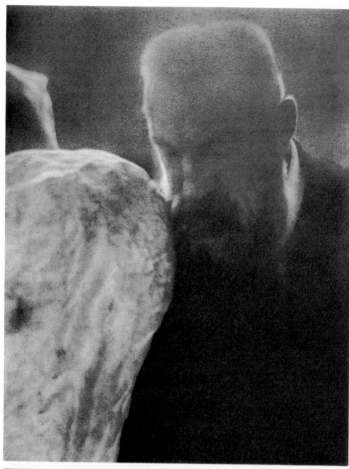

14–15 Auguste Rodin. Paris. 1902. Platinum prints.

16 Rodin—Le Penseur. Paris. 1902. Pigment print.

17 *(above)* Solitude—F. Holland Day. Paris. 1901. Platinum print.
18 *(opposite)* Self Portrait with Brush and Palette. Paris. 1901. Pigment print.

19 Vitality—Yvette Guilbert. Paris. 1901. Pigment print.

20 *(left)* Franz von Lenbach. Munich. 1901. Pigment print.

21 *(right)* Alphons Maria Mucha. Paris. 1901. Platinum print.

22 Edward Everett Hale. Boston. 1903. Pigment print.

23 Maurice Maeterlinck. Paris. 1901. Pigment print.

24 Figure with Iris. Paris. 1902. Pigment print.

25 The Little Round Mirror. Paris. 1902. Platinum print.

26 La Cigale. Paris. 1902. Pigment print.

27 *(below)* Torso. Paris. 1902. Platinum and gum print.

28 *(next page)* In Memoriam. New York. 1904. Platinum and gum print.

After about a year in the rue Boissonade, I returned to the United States. In New York, I looked up Alfred Stieglitz. He took me to the New York Camera Club and introduced me to his friends and to the members. I joined the club, which gave me a place to work. There were wonderful darkroom facilities there, the like of which I had never seen before. At that time, the only serious active photographer around Stieglitz at the Camera Club was Joseph T. Keiley. But Stieglitz had some devoted friends who had stood by him when, as editor of *Camera Notes,* the club's official organ, he had been in conflict with the rank and file members about the contents of the magazine. These dissatisfied members had argued that *Camera Notes* should be devoted to the work of the members of the club and should not be concerned with the art of photography elsewhere.

I was frequently taken to Stieglitz's home at 1111 Madison Avenue for dinner in the evening. His wife, Emmeline, was all cordiality and always urged me to come back soon. At that time, Stieglitz was called "Al" by everyone except his parents; to them, he was always "Alfred." I photographed Stieglitz's enchanting little daughter, "Kitty," with her father (plate 38).

At Stieglitz's home, I was able for the first time to see some of his world-famous photographs. I had seen a few of them in small reproductions in *Camera Notes,* for Stieglitz had sent me several copies while I was still in Paris. Although, in his later years, he refused to enlarge his photographs and even refused to allow reproductions to be made larger than the size of the original, the prints that I saw in his home then were enlargements, quite large and handsomely framed. The place of honor in his home was given to a print titled "The Net Mender." This photograph had taken many prizes in Europe and America. Another prize picture, called "The Letter Box," had been made in Germany. It showed two small children posed in the act of putting a letter in the mail box. But the prints that appealed to me most were "Winter on Fifth Avenue" and "The Hand of Man." "Winter on Fifth Avenue" pictured a horse-drawn bus lumbering through a blizzard on Fifth Avenue. It was entirely different from any photograph I had ever seen. "The Hand of Man" was a picture of a locomotive puffing up big columns of smoke, a sinister, dark image that was very impressive.

Reproductions of paintings that Stieglitz evidently admired in those days were displayed prominently on the walls. They were certainly unlike his photographs. There were two very large reproductions of paintings by Franz Stuck, the German Secessionist painter. One, titled "Sin," was of a standing nude. Around her was coiled a huge snake with threatening eyes. The other was the naked torso of a woman emerging from the body of a sphinx. Her front claws were dripping with blood from the limp body of a man she was embracing. In the same room, there was a famous picture titled "Island of the Dead," by the Swiss painter Arnold Boecklin, and a reproduction of a Lenbach portrait of Eleonora Duse with Lenbach's flaxen-haired child. In the bedroom hung a very handsome photograph of a nude torso by Rubens. Later, in visiting other homes, I found that, in New York in that period, nudes were usually hung in the bedroom.

I met other members of the Stieglitz family, his father and mother, and his brothers and sisters. One of his brothers, Dr. Leopold Stieglitz, took me in charge when health matters were involved. The old gentleman, Edward Stieglitz, Sr., and I developed a very particular and close friendship and mutual affection. I became, in a way, a part of the family. I was, naturally, full of stories about F. Holland Day and the New School exhibitions in London and Paris, but I soon found out that there was a sharp, irreconcilable antagonism between Stieglitz and Day. I stopped singing Day's praises, but began talking about the importance of continually exhibiting photographs.

Naturally, there was also a good deal of talk about the importance of the recent photography exhibition held at the National Arts Club of New York. It was that club's first photography exhibition. Stieglitz had christened it "Photo-Secession" long before anything like an affiliation or organization existed. In fact, no one but Stieglitz seemed to know just what "Photo-Secession" meant. I had been in Paris when this exhibition took place, but I saw photographs of the installation, and they gave a good idea of the quality of the pictures selected. Each photographer's work had been hung as a unit. The over-all impression was rather helter-skelter. At the time, I thought it looked more like a junk shop than an art exhibition.

My next step was to look around for a studio. The

Camera Club was on Thirty-first Street near Fifth Avenue. Around the corner, between Thirtieth and Thirty-first streets, was a block of brownstone fronts, old residences then occupied by small shops and offices. On the top floor of one of these, at 291 Fifth Avenue, I found a small room that was reasonable enough in rent for me to take it over. I had a small, street-level showcase made and hung out my shingle as a professional portrait photographer.

My shingle and showcase on the street, as well as word of mouth between friends and acquaintances, soon commenced to bring in enough portrait work to keep my head above water financially. Also I sold two paintings to Mr. and Mrs. John W. Simpson. Other people, too, were generous with their patronage. There were the Arthur Robinsons, the Roland R. Conklins, the Watson B. Dickermans, and the art dealer Eugene Glaenzer, as well as the entire Stieglitz clan.

A little more than a year after I had made the Rodin portrait, I had my most concentrated and exciting experience in portraiture. In one day I had the job of photographing two great and completely contrasting personalities, J. Pierpont Morgan and Eleonora Duse, within less than an hour's time.

A German portrait painter, Fedor Encke, an old friend of the Stieglitz family, had received a commission to paint an official portrait of J. P. Morgan. Encke found the sittings all too brief and the sitter restive, and the portrait made slow progress. Encke asked Stieglitz to recommend a photographer to help him by making a photograph of Morgan. As a result, Encke commissioned me for the job with the inducement that, if I made a photograph of Morgan in the pose Encke was painting him in, I could also make one for myself. He was certain that I would be recompensed with orders from Morgan or his family. On the day set for the photographing I had the janitor of the studio building take Morgan's place in a chair arranged as in the unfinished Encke painting, so that I might compose the picture on the ground glass in advance.

Morgan arrived with Encke, took off his large hat, laid a foot-long cigar on the edge of a table, sat in the chair previously occupied by the janitor, and took his habitual Encke portrait pose. After a hasty look at the ground glass I said, "Still," and made the two- or three-second exposure required. Then, I took over the making of a negative for myself. I suggested a different position of the hands and a movement of the head. He took the head position, but said, in an irritated tone, that it was uncomfortable, so I suggested he move his head to a position that felt natural. He moved his head several times and ended exactly where it had been "uncomfortable" before, except that this time he took the pose of his own volition. But his expression had sharpened and his body posture became tense, possibly a reflex of his irritation at the suggestion I had made. I saw that a dynamic self-assertion had taken place, whatever its cause, and I quickly made the second exposure, saying, "Thank you, Mr. Morgan," as I took the plate holder out of the camera.

He said, "Is that all?"

"Yes, sir," I answered.

He snorted a reply, "I like you, young man. I think we'll get along first-rate together." Then he clapped his large hat on his massive head, took up his big cigar, and stormed out of the room. Total time, three minutes.

After Encke had escorted Morgan to the elevator, he came back beaming and said that, when Mr. Morgan was about to step into the elevator, he stopped, took out a wad of bills, peeled off five $100 bills and said, "Give this to that young man."

I packed up my equipment and drove to one of the hotels on Fifth Avenue to photograph the immortal Duse (plate 30).

When I developed the negatives of Morgan, I was conscious for the first time of his nose. In the studio, it was his eyes that were the point of focus. But in the photographs, his huge, more or less deformed, sick, bulbous nose seemed now to rivet the attention, and I did not know what to do. What kind of man was Mr. Morgan in this respect? If I should retouch the nose, he might be angry about it. However, the only picture that I had seen reproduced frequently was a portrait of him made by one of the Fifth Avenue photographers in which he had been given a beautiful, neat Roman nose. So I took the negative that I had made for Encke and retouched that nose as much as I dared. On the good negative that I made for myself I did very little retouching, except to make the nose a little more vague and remove spots that were repulsive.

When I took the proofs to Morgan, he thought the one I had retouched for Encke was fine, and he ordered a dozen prints. Then he looked at the other print that I had made for myself. He said, "Terrible," and tore it into shreds. This act of tearing up something that did not belong to him riled my blood. I was not angry because he did not like the picture but because he tore it up. That stung very deep.

I made the twelve prints that he had ordered and sent them to him, but I took the good negative with me when I went back to Paris and made an enlarged negative. Then I worked for a long time before I got what I considered the best possible print (plate 31). The next time I came back to New York, I brought this print along and presented it to Stieglitz. Later he included it in an exhibition of my photographs. Belle Greene, Morgan's librarian, was a constant visitor to 291, and when she saw that print of Morgan, she became very excited. She said it was the best portrait of him that existed in any medium, and she asked Stieglitz to let her take it to show Mr. Morgan.

The next morning she reported that, when she showed the picture to Morgan and told him how wonderful she thought it was, he said he never had seen this picture. Apparently he had forgotten that he had torn up my proof. I will say in extenuation, however, that the relatively small contact print did not have any of the force that this large print had. Morgan told Belle Greene to buy the picture for him. She said she was sure Stieglitz wouldn't sell it, but Morgan said to pay him well for it. He even suggested offering him five thousand dollars, if necessary. Stieglitz, of course, turned down the offer.

When Morgan found out that he couldn't buy that print, he wanted me to make some prints for him. Belle Greene approached me with the request, and I said, "Well, when I get around to it, I'll make some prints for him." For about two years, cablegrams and letters kept arriving, but I ignored them. This was my rather childish way of getting even with Morgan for tearing up that first proof. About three years later, I did make a group of prints for him.

Another sequel to the Morgan portrait came several years later when Pierre Cartier informed me that the Peruvian painter Baca Flor, commissioned to do a portrait of Morgan for the Metropolitan Museum, made a faithful copy of my photograph. My original print, the one that I gave to Stieglitz, is now in the Metropolitan too, a gift of Stieglitz.

Over the years people have referred to the insight into Morgan's real character that I showed by photographing

him with a dagger in his hand. But this was their own fanciful interpretation of Morgan's hand firmly grasping the arm of the chair. It is not only photographers who read meanings into their photographs.

The experience of photographing J. P. Morgan taught me an important lesson. In Milwaukee, I had found that capturing the mood and expression of the moment was more important than photographing the twigs, the leaves, and the branches of the trees. And in photographing the dynamic personality of Morgan, I found that, when he sat in the pose he habitually took for the painter, all I saw was the map of his face, blank and lifeless. But when he was irritated, even by a trifle, something touched the quick of his personality and he reacted swiftly and decisively. The lesson was that a portrait must get beyond the almost universal self-consciousness that people have before the camera. If some moment of reality in the personality of the sitter did not happen, you had to provoke it in order to produce a portrait that had an identity with the person. The essential thing was to awaken a genuine response. This was one of the most valuable lessons I ever learned, and it stood me in good stead later when I worked for *Vanity Fair* and was doing portraits almost daily.

In New York, I had gradually become restive and a little belligerent about the vagueness of the "Photo-Secession." Also, the other photographers who had been represented in the National Arts Club show were urging an organization instead of just a name. As a result, Stieglitz finally set up several informal meetings of the photographers. We decided on an organization with fellows elected either because of their work in photography or because of their real interest in it. There was to be a governing council selected from the fellows. We wanted to make Stieglitz president, but he said that was too ostentatious a title, and he was made director. Thirteen council members were chosen from among the first seventeen fellows nominated. Thirty associate members were also admitted. The full list of founders, fellows, and associates was announced in the July 1903 number of *Camera Work,* along with a statement of the objects and aims of the Photo-Secession. Now the Photo-Secession was a fact, based on a carefully outlined plan.

In the spring of 1905, I learned that a tenant at 293 Fifth Avenue was vacating a larger room that had a big studio skylight. I had just had a very successful exhibition of paintings and felt I could afford the additional rent. I made arrangements with the landlord accordingly to switch my lease from 291 to 293, and since the two buildings shared a central hallway and elevator, I only had to move across the hall.

At the same time, two small rooms were being vacated in the rear of my former studio at 291. The three small rooms together seemed ideal for a gallery for the Photo-Secession, and I commenced talking to Stieglitz about this. At first he demurred. His one strong argument against it was that there wasn't enough important photography being done throughout the world to keep up a continuous exhibition of photographs, but I told him this was not the basic idea. As we had not succeeded in getting photographs hung with paintings in any art gallery, we should try the opposite tack and bring the artists into our sphere. I told him I was sure I could get an exhibition of Rodin drawings and that we might find material for a Salon des Refusés, such as the one held in Paris. This idea intrigued him, and he decided to risk the expense of such an operation.

During that period we had frequent dinner meetings at Mouquin's, a popular French restaurant. All the New York members of the Photo-Secession, plus an occasional out-of-towner, came to these informal meetings. So that we could talk uninterruptedly, we always met upstairs in a private dining room decorated with southern smilax vines. On November 25, 1905, after one of these dinners, the members of the Photo-Secession and their friends went on to 291 Fifth Avenue to witness the fact that the Secession now had a home of its own as well as an organization. On display was a fine show of the members' work. Over the years, the Photo-Secession Galleries came to be referred to as "291."

29 (opposite) Brooklyn Bridge. 1903.

30 *(above)* Eleonora Duse. New York. 1903. Pigment print.

31 *(opposite)* J. P. Morgan. New York. 1903.

32 The Flatiron Building—Evening. New York. 1905. Platinum and ferroprussiate print.

34 *(top)* Cyclamen—Mrs. Philip Lydig. New York. c. 1905. Pigment print.
35 *(bottom)* Mercedes de Cordoba. New York. 1904. Pigment print.

36 Mary and Her Mother. Long Island. 1905. Pigment print.

37 Richard Strauss. New York. 1906. Pigment print.

39 Horse-chestnut Trees. Long Island. 1904. Platinum and gum print.

40 The Big White Cloud. Lake George, New York. 1903. Platinum and gum print.

41 Moonrise—Mamaroneck. New York. 1904. Platinum and ferroprussiate print.

42 Moonrise—New Milford. Connecticut. 1904. Platinum and ferroprussiate print.

43 The Garden of the Gods. Colorado. 1906. Platinum and gum print.

In my studio at 293 Fifth Avenue, across the hall from the Photo-Secession's 291 Gallery, I had been doing quite well as a portrait photographer. As a matter of fact, I began to be troubled when I heard that being photographed by Steichen was considered quite the thing to do. More important, I was dissatisfied with most of the work I was doing, for it had become rather routine. And I found I was getting orders for prints, not from the photographs that I thought were the best, but from the more static, conventional ones. I made up my mind to get away from the lucrative but stultifying professional portrait business, and early in 1906 I packed up my family and moved back to France.

One of the first things I did was to visit Rodin and tell him about the new gallery we had in New York. I told him that we hoped to open our new program with an exhibition of his drawings. He was immensely pleased and promised to let me select whatever I wanted.

Since my promise of a Rodin exhibition had been one of the chief inducements in persuading Stieglitz to open the Photo-Secession Galleries, Stieglitz and I had agreed that the showing of works of art at the Photo-Secession should certainly be inaugurated with this Rodin exhibition. So I was shocked when, in January 1907, I received a formal notice announcing a show of water-color drawings by Pamela Coleman Smith at the Photo-Secession Galleries. It seemed that Stieglitz had jumped the gun on the project I had initiated and on which we had both agreed. I rushed off to the telegraph office and wrote out a telegram to Stieglitz: "Do you still want Rodin drawings?"

In view of the fact that I was paying twenty-five cents a word and had to pay for the address as well as the message, I tried to shorten this telegram. The only thing I could eliminate was the word "still," so the telegram that I finally sent off read, "Do you want Rodin drawings?" This telegram was quoted by several people later on to show that Stieglitz's exhibition of Pamela Smith drawings gave me the idea of sending over the other European things. That saving of twenty-five cents created a long train of confusion.

One day in the summer of 1907, I borrowed from a friend a German hand camera called the Goerzanschutz Klapp Camera. Armed with this camera, I made my first attempt at serious documentary reportage. I went to the Longchamps Races and found an extravagantly dressed society audience, obviously more interested in displaying and viewing the latest fashions than in following the horse races (plates 45 and 46).

The great photographic event of 1907 was the Lumière Company's introduction of color photography in the form of autochrome plates. This was the first practical, direct color photographic process to become available. The results were extraordinary. When Stieglitz and his family arrived in Paris en route to Munich and the Austrian Alps, I showed him the first samples I had made. He was quite excited at the prospect of making direct color photographs, so I got a batch of plates for him to take with him. He and Frank Eugene tried them out later in the summer.

I took some color plates with me to London, where I photographed George Bernard Shaw. Shaw's rosy complexion and luminous blond-red hair and beard made him a natural target for color photography (plate 48). I also photographed a group on a houseboat on the Thames (plate 55), and Lady Ian Hamilton.

When I joined Stieglitz later in Europe and showed him these photographs in color, he wanted them reproduced for *Camera Work*. They were turned over to the Munich firm of Bruckmanns, and that house made marvelous four-color half-tone reproductions for *Camera Work*. (As the original plates are lost, the reproductions in this book have been made from those half-tone reproductions. The fidelity of the reproductions amply testifies to the almost miraculous skill of the engravers.) The curious thing about the autochrome was that, when these plates were turned over to Bruckmanns, the technicians were given no explanation of the autochrome process; they set up the plates, copied them, and, judging from the fine results, had no trouble whatever. A few months later, some scientifically minded German technicians began studying autochrome plates and arrived at the conclusion that, because of their technical color structure, they could not be reproduced. And I believe that was the end of the use of autochrome plates for color reproductions.

The New York public had its first look at my autochrome color photographs during the members' show of the Photo-Secession toward the end of 1907, but Stieglitz showed his autochromes at a press conference as soon as he returned to New York.

Late in the summer of 1908, I received word from Rodin that he had moved his Balzac out into the open air so that I could photograph it. He suggested photographing it by moonlight. I immediately went out to Meudon to see it and found that by daylight the white plaster cast had a harsh, chalky effect. I agreed with Rodin that under the moonlight was the proper way to photograph it. I had no guide to refer to, and I had to guess at the exposure.

I spent the whole night photographing the Balzac. I gave varying exposures from fifteen minutes to an hour, and secured a number of interesting negatives. The three most important results are shown in plates 51, 52, and 53.

In the morning, at breakfast, when I lifted the napkin from my plate, I found two one-thousand franc notes. That was four hundred dollars, a fabulous present for a night's work! It was typical of the generosity of Auguste Rodin. Instead of showing Rodin proofs, I immediately made enlarged negatives and commenced printing.

It wasn't until a week or two later, when I had fine pigment prints, that I turned up to show them to Rodin. The prints seemed to give him more pleasure than anything I had ever done. He said, "You will make the world understand my Balzac through these pictures. They are like Christ walking in the desert."

A few days later, one of his studio helpers came to my place with a beautiful bronze statue called "The Walking Man" ("L'Homme Qui Marche"). When I thanked Rodin, he said the statue was just to show his appreciation and that "L'Homme Qui Marche" was to be a symbol for me of what he hoped my whole life would be—a continuous marching onward.

When Stieglitz saw a set of the Balzac prints later, he seemed more impressed than with any other prints I had ever shown him. He purchased them at once and later presented them to the Metropolitan Museum of Art with most of the other prints of mine that he had acquired by purchase over a number of years. This collection not only represents the major part of the good prints I made during the early periods, but also contains the only surviving record of most of my early work. During World War I, we had to leave my negatives behind, uncared for, in our home in Voulangis when we left. During the four years

of the war, humidity and bacterial action destroyed the emulsions. The plates were ruined.

From the very beginning of my second sojourn in France, I had started to make plans for continuing the exhibitions of modern artists at 291. Like most young Americans in Paris, I had made the acquaintance of the Steins, Gertrude and Leo, as well as the Michael Stein family. At Leo and Gertrude Stein's we could see all types of modern paintings, from Cézanne and Renoir to Matisse and Picasso. Mrs. Michael Stein, a painter herself, bought nothing but Matisses, and her whole apartment was filled with them. It was to her that I first broached the possibility of getting an exhibition of watercolor paintings by Matisse for the Photo-Secession Galleries. She began working on Matisse, and after I met him he promised full cooperation.

There was no difficulty in securing the cooperation of most of the painters, because everybody wanted to exhibit in America. The only real problem was that of space in our galleries. We could handle only small things, drawings and watercolors. Large paintings were out of the question. That is the reason we never showed any of the "Eight's" paintings that were refused at the National Academy. They were all fairly large canvases. Any one of them would probably have covered an entire wall at 291.

Gertrude Stein was instrumental in softening Picasso for us, getting him to agree to a showing at the Photo-Secession in New York. The actual selection of Picasso's contributions for the exhibition in New York was made by the Mexican caricaturist Marius de Zayas and the sculptor Manolo, a compatriot and friend of Picasso's.

About this time, I got to know John Marin. My friend Arthur Carles and I went to the Salon, and in wandering through the section of watercolors, drawings and pastels, we came upon a large group of Marin watercolors, which excited me very much. Carles knew Marin well, and from the Salon we went directly to Marin's studio. I found him as interesting and fine a person as I found his work. However, the real Marin had not yet developed. His watercolors were then more or less realistic and a little reminiscent of Whistler. But I immediately booked Marin for an exhibition at 291.

The following summer, I had Marin come out to our place at Voulangis for a visit. He brought along his watercolor pad and paints. His palette consisted of the ochres, Paines Gray, neutral gray, lamp black, the brown umbers, and Van Dyke browns. I had a watercolor box with all the permanent prismatic colors, *vert émeraude,* rose madder, vermilion, the cadmiums, cobalt, and cerulean blue, and none of the neutral colors. After a certain amount of coaxing, I got him to try my box. He was painting out in the garden, which was full of flowers, and at the first crack a new Marin came out with lovely, vibrant sunlight and color. Marin added these colors to his palette from then on.

When I sent Marin's next exhibition to America, these brighter-colored paintings caused some critics to say he was influenced by Matisse. I don't know any other painter who was so little influenced by the work of anyone else. Certainly none of the Post-Impressionists, Fauves, Cubists, or Cézanne, had any effect on Marin. They simply did not interest him. Everything came out of John Marin himself.

Not long after this I came to realize that the exhibitions of the work of the Society of American Painters in Paris consisted of painters whose work had not developed beyond that of early Impressionism. The society rigorously excluded all the younger and bolder painters from their exhibitions. One evening I invited Marin, Weber, Maurer, Putnam Brinley, and Arthur Carles to my studio, and we discussed forming a new society. After several more meetings, we announced in the Paris edition of the New York *Herald,* and cabled to the New York edition, that the Society of Younger American Painters in Paris had been formed.

The exhibition of the Younger American Painters took place at 291 in 1910. In the same year, I had my last show at the Photo-Secession Galleries, a group of autochrome color photographs. Also in 1910, I brought over an exhibition of etchings and drawings by Gordon Craig, on the art of the theater. Craig was undoubtedly the forerunner of the entire new movement in stage design. With our Paris group, Stieglitz included in the New York Exhibition of Younger American Painters two Americans living in America, Arthur Dove and Marsden Hartley. Marin, Weber, Dove and Hartley have since been recognized as among the most important of that generation of American painters.

In 1910, I made the photograph of Agnes E. Meyer in her wedding dress (plate 44). The first time I met her, she was Agnes Ernst and a reporter on the New York *Sun.* She had come to the Photo-Secession Gallery to write a story about us. Her arrival was an event, for she was not only by far the loveliest girl who had ever been in the gallery, but she was also, in the collective opinion of the Photo-Secessionists, a girl with a mind. From then on, we referred to her as "The Girl from the Sun."

She and de Zayas sold Stieglitz the idea of an avant-garde art magazine called *291.* The three of them became the editorial board of this short-lived but stimulating publication. The Meyers also made possible the one-man show of Brancusi's bronzes and marbles at the 291 Galleries. They paid the cost of packing and shipping the sculptures from Paris to New York and back.

When I commenced to earn money regularly as a photographer on *Vogue* and *Vanity Fair,* it was Eugene Meyer who taught me the importance of saving. By directing the investment of my savings, he laid the groundwork that enabled me to have a modest degree of financial independence today.

After Agnes and Eugene's marriage, the circle of our friendship grew with the arrival of their children. Today it keeps growing with their children's children. When Eugene was dying in 1958, I was at his bedside almost as a member of the family. Agnes and Eugene were exceptionally gifted and intelligent citizens, endowed with sharp social consciences. Theirs was the healthiest and soundest marriage I ever knew.

During the summer of 1910, the Stieglitz family spent a few weeks in Paris on their way to a summer vacation in the Austrian Tyrol. I took Stieglitz around to meet the Steins and Vollard and Durand-Ruel. We also went to the Bernheim Jeune Gallery to see an exhibition of Cézanne watercolors. Stieglitz and I laughed like country yokels as we thought of what a red rag this would be in New York. At the close of the exhibition, I went to the Bernheim Gallery and asked for this exhibition for New York. The fact that we had previously shown Rodin and Matisse made them cooperative. We agreed to have the exhibition during the winter of 1911.

I had been haunted for some time by the idea of testing some of our public, so I painted a fake Cézanne. It was not an imitation of any one picture but a landscape in the style of the Cézanne watercolors. These were all as abstract as anything we had seen in Paris up to that time. In spite of my attempt to make it exactly like the Cézannes, my fake was probably a little more naturalistic. When the exhibition was hung in New York, my fake Cézanne attracted particular attention, possibly because it was more literal.

At any rate, the Cézanne watercolors drew a very hostile response. People "laughed their heads off," critics as well as visitors. Of all the exhibitions we had at 291, this one was probably the most sensational and the most outrightly condemned. Of course, appreciators of avant-garde art thought it was the best we had ever had.

Several people tried to buy my fake, but I explained that it was only on loan and was not for sale. I was petrified by the whole experience. I burned the fake as soon as I could get my hands on it, and only then did I breathe freely again. The "experiment" had given me a clear picture of the snobbery of people who pretended to appreciate things they didn't really understand.

Following Cézanne, we had an exhibition of drawings and watercolors by Picasso. This, in turn, brought a frenzy and a fury into the gallery that eclipsed that of the Cézanne show. It also attracted a few purchasers, among them Stieglitz and Arthur B. Davies, an artist who was a regular and frequent visitor to 291.

In 1912, an exhibition of Arthur Dove's paintings brought a new American name to the public's attention. Next to Marin, Dove was Stieglitz's favorite "wild man" among the young American painters. Stieglitz arranged to have a small income from the sale of his paintings dished out to Dove in regular installments and so practically kept him and his family alive. He made a similar arrangement for Marin, but Marin had had some success from the beginning. This success grew rapidly, until Marin could have sold anywhere, even if there had been no 291 to serve as a showcase for him. This was not the case with Dove's abstractions.

During these winters in New York, I was able to observe the prodigious amount of work that Stieglitz did. His patience was almost unbelievable. With only a brief interruption for lunch, he stood on the floor of the Galleries from ten o'clock in the morning until six or seven o'clock at night. He was always there, talking, talking, talking; talking in parables, arguing, explaining. He was a philosopher, a preacher, a teacher, and a father-confessor. There wasn't anything that wasn't discussed openly and continuously in the Galleries at 291. If the exhibitions at 291 had been shown in any other art gallery, they would never have made an iota of the impact that they did at 291. The difference was Stieglitz.

The audience, especially the regulars, learned a great deal from Stieglitz at 291, but no one learned as much there as Stieglitz did himself. People who came to 291 enriched Stieglitz, and as long as they did, he was their friend. Max Weber was the first one to argue Stieglitz into seeing that Stieglitz's early work was much better than his later "pictorial" work. De Zayas took up this argument further. It was de Zayas who found among Stieglitz's proofs a "Steerage" picture, which Stieglitz had overlooked. The "Steerage" picture that Stieglitz had selected and reproduced in *Camera Work* was not nearly so fine as the one that later became his most famous and popular photograph.

But Stieglitz only tolerated people close to him when they completely agreed with him and were of service. Gertrude Käsebier was the first Photo-Secessionist to be forced out of the organization, because she was antagonistic to some of the things that Stieglitz did. Next was Clarence White, for the same reason. Stieglitz unjustly tried to claim that these two were jealous of other photographers and of the attention being given to the artists. The next person to be expelled was Max Weber. Weber was a little fighting cock; what he believed in was sacred to him, and he fought Stieglitz tooth and nail. The relationship became intolerable to both. Stieglitz never forgave Weber, and to the end of his days, he expressed himself bitterly about him.

Stieglitz's greatest legacy to the world is his photographs, and the greatest of these are the things he began doing toward the end of the 291 days.

44 Agnes E. Meyer (Mrs. Eugene Meyer). New York. 1910. Pigment print.

45 Steeplechase Day, Paris: Grandstand. 1905. Pigment print.

46 Steeplechase Day, Paris: After the Races. 1905. Pigment print.

47 The Photographer's Best Model—George Bernard Shaw. London. 1907. Platinum print.

48 George Bernard Shaw. London. 1907. From Lumière Autochrome reproduced here
from the four-color half-tone published in *Camera Work,* April, 1908.

49 Mary and Kate Steichen. Voulangis, France. 1913.

50 *(above)* Rodin. Paris. 1910. Platinum print.

(next two pages) Balzac:

51 *(left top)* Towards the Light, Midnight. Meudon. 1908. Pigment print.

52 *(left bottom)* The Silhouette, 4 a.m. Meudon. 1908. Pigment print.

53 *(right)* The Open Sky. Meudon. 1908. Pigment print.

54 Henri Matisse (and «La Serpentine»). Issy-les-Moulineaux. 1909. Platinum print.

55 Houseboat on the Thames. 1907. From Lumière Autochrome reproduced
here from the four-color half-tone published in *Camera Work,* April, 1908.

56 *(opposite)* President Theodore Roosevelt. The White House. 1908. Pigment print. For *Everybody's Magazine*.

57 *(below)* William Howard Taft. Washington, D.C. 1908. Pigment print. For *Everybody's Magazine*.

58 Mrs. Conde Nast. Paris. 1907. Pigment print.

59 Nocturne—Orangerie Staircase, Versailles. c. 1910. Pigment print.

60 Lotus. Mount Kisco, New York. 1915. Palladium print.

62 Heavy Roses. Voulangis, France. 1914. Palladium print.

At the outbreak of the war in France in the autumn of 1914, everyone's life changed within twenty-four hours. War became the dominating theme. Firstline conscripts who had to go the first day were followed by those who went on the second day, and so on. Horses were requisitioned, and every foreigner was suspected as a spy. Even some French people were suspected.

As the German Army commenced to move toward Paris, it was rumored that communiqués were always two or three days late in reporting the facts. It was so difficult to know the situation that I finally sent a cautious cable to Eugene Meyer in New York: "What do you advise?"

A prompt reply came back: "Advise strategic retreat." So we retreated. We got out of our place two days before an advance patrol of German troops arrived. Later, a British cavalry troop was encamped on what had been my delphinium field.

Back in New York, I found the Photo-Secession in the doldrums. An exhibition of African sculpture collected by de Zayas was on display. The burlap walls were dust-covered, and there was a dust-covered atmosphere about the whole place. No one came but the few 291'ers. I asked Stieglitz to let me brighten up that fine exhibition, and he agreed. I bought several reams of yellow, orange, and black sheets of paper. I took all the sculptures down and made an abstract geometrical pattern on the walls with the gay-colored papers, then put the sculptures back in place. The whole room came alive, the colored papers serving like a background of jungle drums. We all seemed in somewhat better spirits when Stieglitz said, "Well, what are you going to do after this?" I told him this was the first time he had ever questioned me as to what I was going to do.

We had a few drawings by Braque and Picasso, and I determined that they would be fine material for the next exhibition. I bought some bolts of cheesecloth, the cheapest I could find, and we covered the dust-darkened burlap walls with it. A lad by the name of Zoler, who had become a sort of shadow to Stieglitz, helped me pin up the cheesecloth. I took down the denim curtains hiding our storage shelves and sent them out to be dyed black. Then I hung the few Braques and Picassos on the walls and several of the more or less related African sculptures with them. The place looked clean, fresh, and alive again, but I felt some-

thing was missing. The exhibition needed a real object, a stone or a piece of wood or something. When I mentioned this, Zoler said he had a big wasp's nest in fine condition. A wasp's nest was perfect, especially in relationship to the Cubism we had on the wall, and it was brought in. The exhibition inspired my friend Charles Sheeler to make a couple of his finest photographs.

The arrival of Picabia from Paris shortly after marked the beginning of an influx to New York of European artists and their champions, and the exhibitions took on a different character. The Dadaism of Picabia did not interest me. I felt it was not a time for mockery and discouragement, and I took no part in the shows. As a matter of fact, I took part in few of the remaining exhibitions.

It was obvious, with a world at war, that there was not going to be a lively interest in the arts. The audiences at 291 were few and far between. I felt that we should broaden our work into something that could lead to our becoming a civilizing force in the world. Among our regular visitors were poets and musicians, and I advocated their inclusion as fellows of the Photo-Secession. There was young Alfred Kreymborg, with his avant-garde poetry, and there was the composer Edgar Varèse, a musician of extraordinary depth and originality. I felt that these people, representing the other arts, belonged in 291. The Photo-Secession was really dead, and I thought we should have a new organization.

Stieglitz, however, was interested in a project of self-adulation. He was preparing a special number of *Camera Work* devoted to the question, "What is 291?" He asked everybody to write his personal version of what 291 represented. As might be expected, especially from his way of presenting the project, most of the versions stated that 291 was Stieglitz. In a larger sense, this was true. But I, with dreams of the Photo-Secession becoming something greater and more meaningful, wrote the only sharp minority opinion. I said, in part:

"291? I have never known just what it was, I don't know now, and I do not believe anyone else does. 291 only seems to us what we as individuals want it to be, and because I have my particular 'want it to be' stronger today than ever before, do I resent this inquiry into its meaning as being impertinent, egoistic and previous. Previous in so far that it makes the process resemble an obituary or an inquest, and because it further tends to establish a precedent in the form of a past....

"It can never have anything resembling a constitution or an eternal policy, for the very good reason that any one of these would be sufficient to dull its receptivity to new elements, especially to the one element which has ever arrived opportunely and kept 291 a living issue:—the great unforeseen.... Therefore, there is no permanent room for dogma or even the trace of anything that moves toward dogma.

"During the past year, possibly two years, 291 has seemed to me to be merely marking time. It had obviously reached a result in one of its particular efforts and had accomplished a definite result within itself and for itself:— and for the public at large it had laid the way for others to successfully organize the big International Exhibition of Modern Art held at the Armory in 1913....

"Again arrives the unforeseen—came the war....

"291 continued the process of producing a book about itself—and calmly continued its state of marking time. As 291 it had failed for once, and on this, an occasion of the greatest necessity, to realize its relationship to the great unforeseen.... By this failure it still left many individuals outside of its immediate circle riding about with the solemn conviction that 291 was merely a 'rival to the old Camera Club' or 'Mr. Stieglitz's Gallery for the newest in art.'"

The exhibitions continued, with two new and important notes. One day a roll of drawings arrived, addressed to Stieglitz, and we all looked at them. We were dumbfounded. They were a batch of charcoal drawings by Georgia O'Keeffe. In these abstract drawings was a woman who spoke with amazing psychological frankness of herself as a woman. A show of Paul Strand's photographs was the other new American note at 291.

When it was indicated that America would sooner or later become involved in the war, the Galleries were closed with a final exhibition of the more recent work of Georgia O'Keeffe. She later became the wife of Stieglitz.

Stieglitz and I differed as to what the future of 291 could be, and we also differed in our feelings about the war. Through the years, France had become another mother country to me, and I sided with her in all the arguments with Stieglitz. The climax came with the sinking of the *Lusitania*. When Stieglitz said, "It served them right.

They were warned in advance that the ship would be sunk," I decided then and there that I wanted to get into the war on the American side. I wanted to be a photographic reporter, as Mathew Brady had been in the Civil War, and I went to Washington to offer my services, with the endorsement of the Camera Clubs of America.

When I found that the Signal Corps was charged with photography, I went to them and was accepted. Two news photographers were accepted at the same time, and the three of us were given the rank of lieutenant. The chief of the Signal Corps told us that the best man would be placed in charge. But a few days later, a Major Barnes was brought into the Signal Corps Photographic Section and, as ranking officer, was placed in charge. Then Major Campbell, an English aerial photographer, was sent over to coach us. The Air Service also was a part of the Army Signal Corps, and when I learned from Major Campbell about the importance of aerial photography, I became very much interested.

Major Barnes selected me to go to France with him as his technical adviser in organizing the work over there. All he knew about photography was whatever he had learned on a hunting safari when he made a motion picture of wild animals. We set off for France with the first convoy of American troops in a seized German liner.

When we landed at Cherbourg and received the first newspapers, I read on the front page of Rodin's death the day before. This news ended a dream I had had of calling on him in my uniform as a symbol of America coming over to help France. When we arrived in Paris, I immediately started pulling strings to be sent to Rodin's funeral as a representative of the American Army. It could not be done officially in such a short time, but Major Barnes said, "Sure, you go and you say that you represent the American Army and General Pershing." When I got there, I added that I also represented the Younger American Artists.

The funeral was held at Meudon, and there was a great crowd of Academicians as well as Rodin's friends. The Academicians, the men who had always fought Rodin and ridiculed him, were there in frock coats to present eulogies, stuffed-shirt talks about "La Gloire de l'Art Français." Clemenceau had ordered a platoon of French *poilus* back from the front as a guard of honor. Overhead, French fighter planes kept vigil in the sky. Several hundred people had come to see Rodin buried alongside his beloved and loyal Rose, at the feet of the large bronze statue of "Le Penseur."

After all the officials had made their speeches, a woman rose unannounced and made a wonderful, fervid speech about Rodin as an artist and as one who understood humanity and womankind particularly. It was a startling deviation from the official ceremony, the only human note, the only thing honestly said about the man and the artist Rodin.

I met a number of old acquaintances at the funeral, among them Judith Cladel. As she told it, Rodin's official marriage to Rose a few days before her death, and those very last days, which came only a few days after Rose's burial, were one of the most ghastly experiences anybody could have gone through. Fortunately, he was in a semi-coma during much of this time. The activities of schemers around him representing the state, and individuals conspiring to get control of his work through various wills, were among the ugliest things that ever happened to any artist, let alone an artist considered one of the greatest geniuses that France had produced.

Major Barnes gave me a short leave of absence, with orders to proceed to the British front and study aerial photography. What I learned convinced me that my duty was with the Air Service, and I had myself transferred from the Historical Section of the Signal Corps to the Photographic Section of the Air Service. Major Barnes was still in charge. We moved our base of operations from Paris to General Pershing's headquarters at Chaumont. Soon the general's staff was consulting me about everything photographic, and Major Barnes was sent back to the States to take charge of the School of Aerial Photography in Rochester, New York, while I ran things in France.

During the Second Battle of the Marne, which was the first time American Forces were engaged, I met General Billy Mitchell. The first question he asked me after the formal introduction was, "When are we going to get any ninety centimeter cameras for the high-altitude photography?"

I said, "Sir, we have six already."

"Well, why aren't they in use?"

I explained that the pilots in the observation squadrons objected to them because they took up so much room that the gunner was not free to work his gun.

"Well, can you get one out here?" General Mitchell asked me. "I'll take it up."

A camera was delivered to him from our supply depot in Paris the same day.

After asking me several questions about aerial photography processing, General Mitchell seemed convinced that I knew what I was talking about and that I understood the urgent need for equipment and materials. He put in an order for me to be attached to his service during each important military operation.

The next time I met General Mitchell was just before our great Meuse-Argonne offensive. He called our office at the advance air base, Colombey-les-belles. As I was out on a tour of inspection, he told my adjutant that he wanted a photographic truck and a working photographic section out at a certain place in a brewery building by the next morning. Prints of the French Intelligence photographs of the Argonne front would be needed urgently.

My adjutant was an able man. He rounded up everybody who had ever developed a negative or been an amateur snap-shotter, along with one or two of our experienced laboratory men. When I got back to my office at Colombey-les-belles, he informed me that the personnel and the equipment trailer had gone. I drove out over the same route and found they had set up darkroom space, connected water and electricity from the truck generator, gotten the negatives, and were at work making prints.

I asked them to keep at it as long as they could. They had to make fifty prints from each of these thousands of negatives for distribution to headquarters and the front lines. At five o'clock in the morning, I went back to the lab and found them still working. I think that if one of those boys had said he was tired and wanted to quit, the others would have lynched him.

At seven o'clock, I went out to see whether I couldn't scrounge some breakfast for them. Walking down the street toward me was General Mitchell, jaunty as ever, swagger stick slapping his boots as he went along. I saluted him, and he asked me sharply if we had gotten that truck and outfit there.

"Yes sir," I replied. "They're working."

"When will we have some prints?" he asked.

"We delivered the first five thousand this morning," I said.

All he said was "Good," and he walked on. From then on I had a friend in General Billy Mitchell.

On November 11, 1918, came the Armistice. The wholesale murdering was over, and wild celebrations began that night: cheering, yelling, screaming, booze, noise.

I went into my room at the barracks and flung myself on the bed. The whole monstrous horror of the war seemed to fall down on me and smother me. I smelled the rotting carcasses of dead horses, saw the three white faces of the first American dead that I had seen. I could hear the rat-a-tat-tat of machine-gun fire as one lay flat on one's belly trying to dig into the earth to escape it, and the ping-ping-ping of the bullets coming through the leaves overhead. I saw the dried blood around the bullet hole in a young soldier's head. And he was only one of hundreds of thousands. How could men and nations have been so stupid? What was life for if it had to end like this? What was the use of living?

I had never had to come face to face with another man and shoot him and see him crumple up and fall, yet I could not deny to myself having played a role in the slaughter. I had never been conscious of anything but the job we had to do: photograph enemy territory and enemy actions, record enemy movements and gun emplacements, pinpoint the targets for our own artillery. The work had been full of organizational and technical difficulties. We had had to improvise all along the way with inadequate equipment and materials and inadequately trained personnel. But the photographs we made provided information that, conveyed to our artillery, enabled them to destroy their targets and kill.

A state of depression remained with me for days, but gradually there came a feeling that, perhaps, in the field of art, there might be some way of making an affirmative contribution to life. This thought restored some sanity and hope, and the desire to live took hold again.

When I finally returned to my house and garden at Voulangis, I entered a time of deep, earnest soul-searching that led to three of the most productive years of my life. I began by painting a few pictures of the flowers growing in my garden. One morning, when I went to my studio, I found a very free copy of a flower painting I had been working on. The copy was painted on my palette from the colors I had been using the day before. It had been done by the gardener, a Brittany peasant, and it had the curious charm and direct simplicity of much primitive painting. As such, it was better than what I had been trying to do. This discovery suddenly crystallized the problem I had been worrying about ever since the Armistice. I knew now what I really wanted to do.

I called the gardener, and we pulled all the paintings out of my studio into an open area and made a bonfire. I was through with painting. Painting meant putting everything I felt or knew into a picture that would be sold in a gold frame and end up as wallpaper. The statement I had made so spontaneously to Stieglitz in 1900, "I will always stick to photography!" rang in my ears. It was true. Photography was to be my medium. I wanted to reach into the world, to participate and communicate, and I felt I would be able to do this best through photography. I decided on another apprenticeship. I would learn how to make photographs that could go on the printed page, for now I was determined to reach a large audience instead of the few people I had reached as a painter.

The wartime problem of making sharp, clear pictures from a vibrating, speeding airplane ten to twenty thousand feet in the air had brought me a new kind of technical interest in photography completely different from the pictorial interest I had had as a boy in Milwaukee and as a young man in Photo-Secession days. Now I wanted to know all that could be expected from photography.

One of my experiments has become a sort of legend. It consisted of photographing a white cup and saucer placed on a graduated scale of tones from pure white through light and dark grays to black velvet. This experiment I did at intervals over a whole summer, taking well over a thousand negatives. The cup and saucer experiment was to a photographer what a series of finger exercises is to a pianist. It had nothing directly to do with the conception or the art of photography.

There were other things I wanted to learn. I was particularly interested in a method of representing volume, scale, and a sense of weight. Growing in espalier fashion on the walls of my garden were trees that produced fine, large apples and pears. On them were a few particularly good specimens. I used these apples and pears in my attempts to render volume and weight. At first it made no difference how I placed the fruit. Whether they were in direct sunlight, as in plate 63, or in interiors, I did not get the feeling of volume. But I noticed that diffused light came closer to giving the desired result. In my small greenhouse I constructed a tent of opaque blankets, put a single apple inside, and cut off all direct light. From a tiny opening not larger than a nickel, I directed light against one side of the covering blanket, and this light, reflected from the blanket, was all. Then, to get as much depth as possible, I made a small diaphragm that must have been roughly f128. I removed some of the blankets to compose and focus the picture, replaced them, and made a series of exposures that ran from six hours to thirty-six. The most successful ones took thirty-six hours. But something happened that I hadn't counted on.

The fact that the longer exposures lasted more than two days and one night meant that, as the nights were cool, everything, including the camera and the covering, contracted and the next day expanded. Instead of producing one meticulously sharp picture, the infinitesimal movement produced a succession of slightly different sharp images, which optically fused as one (plates 64 and 65). Here for the first time in a photograph, I was able to sense volume as well as form. What was more, when both pictures were enlarged to four by five feet, the scale or actual size of the objects represented became unimportant. This elimination of the realistic element of scale made abstract images of these photographs.

The "Wheelbarrow with Flower Pots" (plate 67) was certainly as realistic a photograph as I had ever made. Yet, friends remarked that it made them think of one thing or another that had nothing to do with the wheelbarrow and the flower pots. They thought of "heavy artillery" and "log jams," for example. I began to reason that, if it was possible to photograph objects in a way that makes them suggest something entirely different, perhaps it would be possible to give abstract meanings to very literal photographs. I made many pictures exploring the idea.

One of them involved something I was deeply absorbed in trying to understand, because it was being discussed a great deal at the time. It was Einstein's Theory of Relativity. One angle that was particularly intriguing was Einstein's "Time-Space Continuum." I tried to express this concept by using objects as symbols (plate 68). I did a whole series with eggs and another with a harmonica and a glass bell used by gardeners for protecting plants from frost in early spring (plate 69). But in trying these things

out on the same friends who had responded with so much imagination to the "Wheelbarrow with Flower Pots," I found they were completely bewildered. Not understanding the symbolic use to which I was putting the objects, they had no clue to the meaning of the pictures. I began to realize that abstraction based on symbols was feasible only if the symbols were universal. Symbols that I invented as I went along would not be understood by anyone but myself.

One thing that had been bothering me in relation to the whole Post-impressionist movement in painting was that this was the first period in the history of art that lacked a basic discipline as its general point of departure. The artist now recognized only what he as an individual artist conceived as discipline in connection with his own painting or sculpture. Vividly remembering how often Rodin had spoken of going to nature for inspiration, I felt it might be possible to go to nature to find a discipline. I recalled the words Rodin had written for the opening page of the number of *Camera Work* devoted to my own work, the same issue for which the Maeterlinck article had been written. Rodin had said, *"Quand on commence à comprendre la nature, les progrès ne cessent plus."* (When one begins to understand nature, progress goes on unceasingly.)

So I set out to try to understand nature's discipline. I decided to make a study of the ratio of plant growth and structure. For many years, I had been impressed by the beauty of the spiral shell on the snails so abundant in our garden. Even the tiniest snail carried a house constructed in the perfect geometric form of a spiral. I found some form of the spiral in most succulent plants and in certain flowers, particularly in the seed pods of the sunflower, of which I had made so many photographic studies (plates 75 to 78). I decided there must be a relationship between all these things and what had been known for a long time as the Golden Section, or Golden Measure: the proportion of extreme and mean ratio. Plato had referred to this proportion as "the section."

I went searching for books and found, among other things, that Leonardo had been interested in the Golden Section and Goethe had been intrigued by the spiral. I studied plane and solid geometry and learned how to use a slide rule to calculate the proportions and relationships of the forms that interested me. Finally I found a book written in 1914 by Theodore Andrea Cooke, *The Curves of*

Life, Being an Account of Spiral Formations and Their Application to Growth in Nature. This book not only confirmed the vague findings I had struggled so hard to determine, but also covered things I had never dreamed of. It discussed the spiral in shells and plants, went on to trace its significant use in architecture, and reported all of Leonardo's findings relating the growth of the spiral to the proportions of the human body. And, what was flabbergasting to me, the book also contained reproductions of astronomical photographs of the spiral nebulae in the heavens. From that time on I began to feel sure that, one day, scientists would discover that the shape of the universe itself was the logarithmic spiral. If only I had found his book earlier, Cooke's detailed scientific investigations could have saved me months of laborious study and calculation.

The revelation of Cooke's writings on spiral formations in nature was still upon me when my friend Arthur Carles, who knew of the work I was doing, sent me some copies of a magazine called *The Diagonal,* written and edited entirely by Jay Hambidge and published by the Yale University Press. Hambidge had worked out the problem of the "section" in a geometric form in which he used a square to produce a series of rectangles. One rectangle was in mean and extreme ratio, the others built upon it were a series of root rectangles.

Hambidge's findings led him to believe that the rectangle in the proportion of root 5 was the most important and beautiful form, and he claimed that it was the basis of the Parthenon and the Greek vases. Hambidge's work and theories have been lost sight of, but during his lifetime his system of the diagonal was applied by George Bellows and several other painters. I felt, however, that it could not logically be applied to realistic painting, because it would involve imposing a two-dimensional symmetry on a three-dimensional representation.

In my work, I started with Hambidge's rectangle and divided the area into three triangles, each of which was still, of course, in extreme and mean ratio, or the Golden Mean. This proportion can also be stated mathematically as a ratio of .618 to 1.618.

In experimenting with the three triangles I had cut out, I was fascinated with the curious shapes that could be formed, and I started using these shapes as the subject matter for a children's story I wanted to do. I called the images evoked by assembling the three triangles *The Oochens.* Oochens lived in a special kind of imaginary republic, of which an Oochen named Khor was the President. Some of the other characters were Thinkrates, the Philosopher; Mushton-Slushley, the Lyric Poet; and the Pink Faced Politician, who always wept because the world was going to the dogs. There was also a lovely creature I called the Radio Gull, a streamlined composition of the three basic triangles in white against a blue ground. In the story, the Radio Gull was the messenger of Khor, carrying Khor's thoughts to any part of the republic in an instant.

There was a curious coincidence about Theodore Cooke's book, *The Curves of Life.* It had as a frontispiece a reproduction of Rodin's "Le Penseur." Beneath it was this beautiful statement by Rodin about nature: "*La Nature c'est le modèle variable et infini qui contient tous les styles. Elle nous entoure mais nous ne la voyons pas.*" (Nature is the infinite and variable model that contains all styles. She surrounds us, but we do not see her.) As I worked on the Golden Measure or Golden Section, I discovered that everything growing outdoors had become exceptionally alive to me. In the small tempera paintings I made of the Oochens, I experienced a sense of freedom I had never experienced before in painting. I believe it came from the knowledge that I was doing something based on nature's laws. The inexorable discipline gave me a new kind of freedom.

63 Pear on a Plate. France. c. 1920.

64 *(opposite)* Three Pears and an Apple. France. c. 1921.

65 *(above)* An Apple, a Boulder, a Mountain. France. c. 1921.

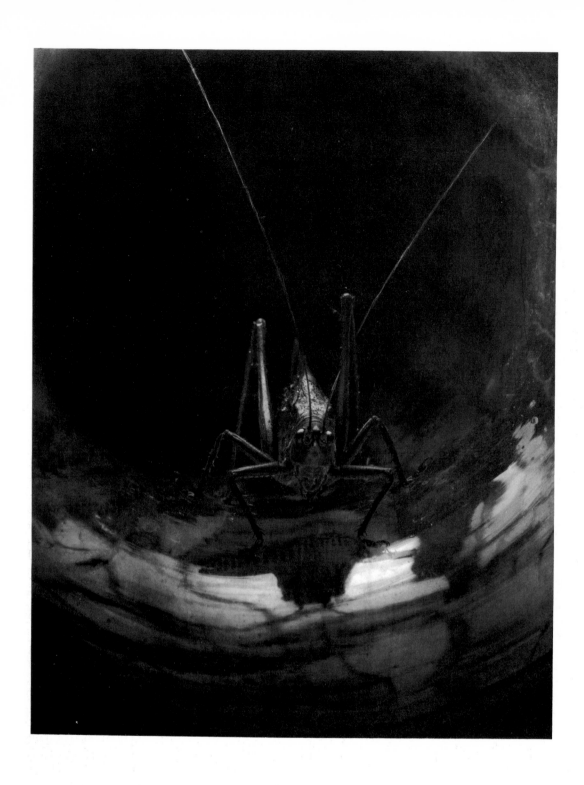

66 Diagram of Doom —1. France. c. 1921.

67 Wheelbarrow with Flower Pots. France. 1920. Palladium and ferroprussiate print.

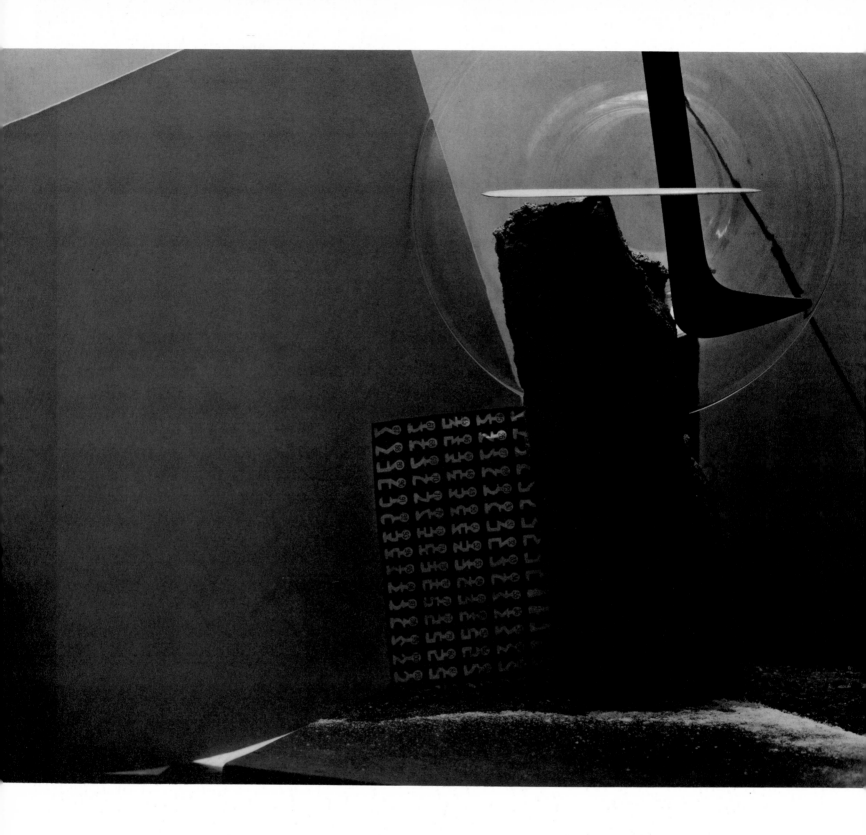

68 *(above)* "Time-Space Continuum." France. c. 1920.

69 *(opposite)* Harmonica Riddle. France. c. 1921. Palladium print.

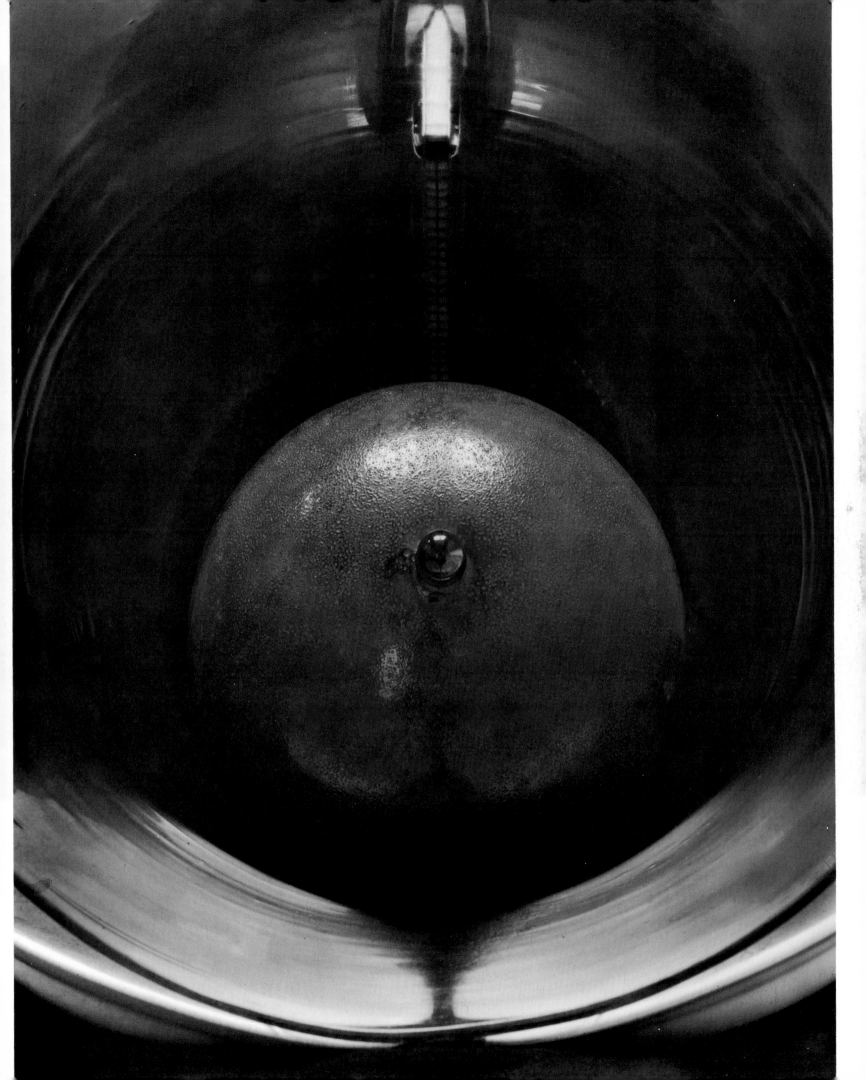

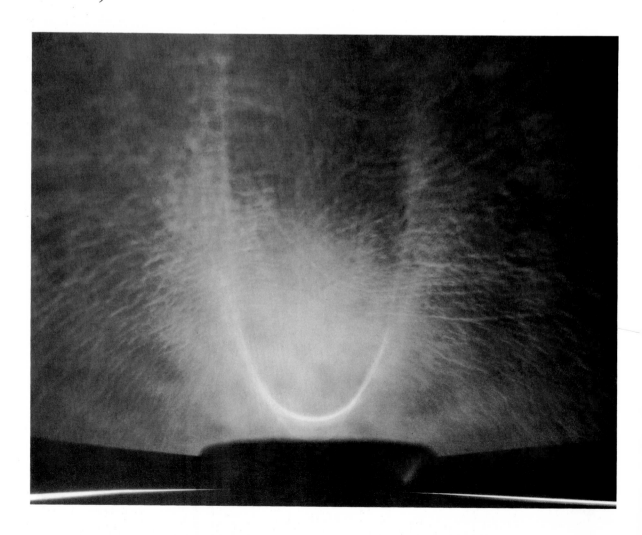

70 *(top)* "Triumph of the Egg." France. c. 1921. Palladium print.

71 *(bottom)* From the Outer Rim. France. c. 1921.

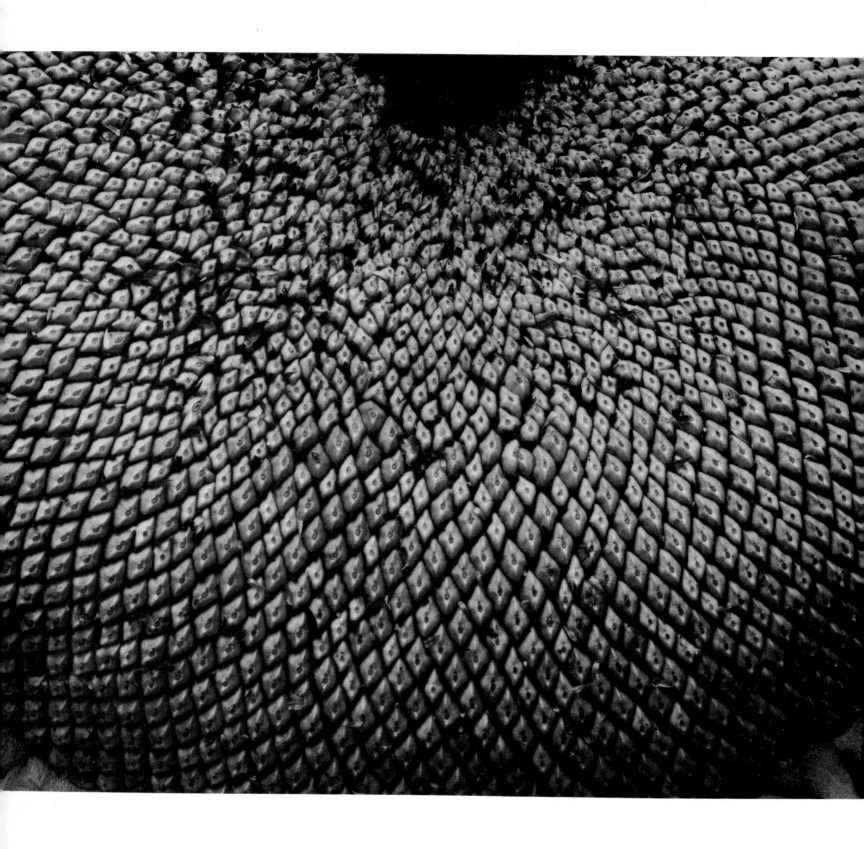

75 *(above)* Sunflower in Seed. Part of a series—"From Seed to Seed"
—begun in France in 1920 and still in progress.

76 *(opposite)* Aging Sunflower.

77 *(opposite)* A Bee on a Sunflower.

78 *(above)* Backbone and Ribs of a Sunflower.

79 *(above)* Frozen Begonia Plant. France. c. 1922.

80 *(opposite)* Foxgloves. France. 1926.

81 Raindrops. France. c. 1920.

82 *(above)* Frost on Rambler Roses. Voulangis, France. 1920.

83 *(next page)* E. Gordon Craig; Notre Dame de Paris. 1920. Palladium print.

In 1921, when I had worn myself to a frazzle on the problems connected with the spiral and the extreme and mean ratio, as well as on the photographic problems, I decided on a brief vacation. I started for Venice with the intention of spending a week or ten days flat on my back in a gondola.

My train arrived in Venice at night, and I took a gondola to the hotel. Crossing the Grand Canal, I heard some gay voices, one of which I thought I recognized as Isadora Duncan's. I had the gondolier go over toward the sound of the voices, and I found that it really was Isadora, with her pianist, Walter Rummel, and her pupils, who were generally referred to as the Isadorables. These pupils were all German girls adopted by Isadora when they were children. As well as teaching them dancing, she provided them with an excellent education. When my gondola pulled up alongside Isadora's, there were the screams and gaieties of greeting, and Isadora immediately said, "We are leaving for Greece early tomorrow morning. You must come along."

Well, then and there a specific plan for a vacation was replaced by a better one. Early the next morning, the whole crowd was on a steamer bound for Greece.

What little knowledge I had of Greece came from books, the "Venus de Milo" and other Greek statues in the Louvre, and the fragments of sculpture from the Parthenon in London; but soon I found myself looking from the windows of a hotel in Athen at the Acropolis, crowned by the Parthenon. The most kind sunlight and the smells of the hot, baking land differed from anything I had ever experienced.

The real argument with which Isadora persuaded me to go along to Greece was that we could borrow a motion-picture camera when we got there, and she would let me make motion pictures of her dancing on the Acropolis. When we got to Athens, she changed her mind. She said she didn't want her dancing recorded in motion pictures but would rather have it remembered as a legend. However, she did promise to pose for me for some still photographs. So I borrowed a Kodak camera from the headwaiter at the hotel, and we made several trips up the Acropolis to the Parthenon. But, every time, she said she couldn't do it; it was too much; she felt like an intruder when she started to move.

Finally, one day, I coaxed her into standing in the portal of the Parthenon. The camera was set up far enough away to include the whole portal wall. The idea was that she was to do her most beautiful single gesture, the slow raising of her arms until they seemed to encompass the whole sky. She stood there for perhaps fifteen minutes, saying, "Edward, I can't. I can't do it. I can't do it here." But finally, after several tries, I saw the arms going up. This was the moment. Fortunately, the camera was ready. I waited to catch a particular instant near the apex of the movement (plate 86). Then we went around to the portico with its line of columns. She removed her cloak and stood there in her Greek tunic. And here she contributed what only an artist like Isadora could contribute. She made a gesture completely related to the columns (plate 85).

That visit to the Parthenon was the only time Isadora posed for photographs there. She always said she was so completely overwhelmed by what she felt there that she could not pose. Her whole art of dancing was inspired by the Greek architectural friezes and the drawings on Greek vases. She was a part of Greece, and she took Greece as a part of herself.

I did have several sessions on the Acropolis with Isadora's pupils, particularly with Thérèse, who was, I felt, the most talented of them. Unlike Isadora, Thérèse had no feelings of conflict. She was a living reincarnation of a Greek nymph. Once, while photographing the Parthenon, I lost sight of her, but I could hear her. When I asked where she was, she raised her arms in answer. I swung the camera around and photographed her arms against the background of the Erechtheum (plate 84). And then we went out to a part of the Acropolis behind the Parthenon, and she posed on a rock, against the sky with her Greek garments. The wind pressed the garments tight to her body, and the ends were left flapping and fluttering. They actually crackled. This gave the effect of fire—"Wind Fire" (plate 87).

During the postwar years, I made several trips to New York. On one of those trips, I made photographs from the windows of the apartment where I lived. Three of them are in plates 88, 89, and 90. I also made the acquaintance of Dana Desboro, a young actress, and made a series of photographs of her (plates 91, 92, and 93). We were married in 1923.

Plate 89, of Dana Steichen and the apple, is an example of a two-color process I had been working on for several years and later used for *Vogue* and *Vanity Fair*. The two-color negatives were produced by two different emulsions of film, one red-sensitive, one blue-sensitive, used as a bi-pack. When these two negatives were printed, one in orange-red, the other in green-blue, the effect was close to a full three-color photograph, but I usually printed one in brown instead of bright red and the other in blue or black, as in the duotone plates 65 and 196. The plate "Dana and the Apple" was reproduced from a print in which one color was printed in terra-cotta red and the second color in Prussian blue.

The photograph "Mr. and Mrs.: the Sandburgs" (plate 94) was made during this period too. I first met Carl Sandburg in 1907, when my sister brought him to visit my parents. They were married shortly after. I have always felt that, when my little sister acquired a husband, I acquired a brother. For with that marriage, there began a warm, close friendship, which has remained fruitful and wonderful for both Carl and me to this day. We shared in each other's dreams and aspirations and formed something of a mutual admiration society. I designed the jacket of

Carl's first published book of poems, and Carl wrote the first "biography of a photographer." Called *Steichen the Photographer,* it was published by Harcourt, Brace and Company in 1929, and later reprinted in part in Carl's book *The Sandburg Range* in 1957. When the Museum of Modern Art gave me a retrospective exhibition in 1961, Carl's title, *Steichen the Photographer,* was used again. In 1942, we collaborated on "Road to Victory," the first large-scale exhibition I did for The Museum of Modern Art; I selected the pictures and organized the exhibition, and Carl wrote the text.

When Carl Sandburg wrote *The People, Yes,* the greatest of his poems, he not only became the poet of the American people, he also created the outstanding image that has been made of Americans. I remember one day in Greece, when Isadora, her pupils, Walter Rummel, and I were headed up to the Parthenon. We stopped at a place on the road that had an abutment from which, it is said, Pericles addressed the multitude. I stepped out on this platform and recited Carl's poem about Billy Sunday. My little audience ended up in roars of laughter. Then Isadora came up and said, "That's wonderful, but is it poetry?" Isadora's concept of poetry did not get much beyond the Greeks.

If I were to make a list of the major American artists of our time, I would head the list with the names of Carl Sandburg and Frank Lloyd Wright.

84 *(below)* Thérèse Duncan: Reaching Arms. The Parthenon. 1921.

(next two pages)

85 *(left)*   Isadora Duncan—Columns of the Parthenon. 1921.

86 *(right)*   Isadora Duncan at the Portal of the Parthenon. 1921.

87 Wind Fire: Thérèse Duncan on the Acropolis. 1921.

88 Milk Bottles: Spring, New York. 1915.

89 Sunday Papers: West 86th Street, New York. c. 1922.

90 Laughing Boxes: West 86th Street, New York. c. 1922.

92 *(opposite)* Dana and the Apple. New York. 1922. Two-color process and print.
"We have bitten the apple, tasted the bite of the apple, made
known to our tongue the taste of the apple; it is set
before us with pride, arrogance; our eyes carry a challenge;
what do you care?"
                                                    Carl Sandburg

91 *(below)* Dana's Hands and Grasses. Long Island, New York. 1923. Palladium print.
"Startled gazelles; so we might say; only these two forearms
and wrist joints and testifying fingers are all writhing
too eagerly."
                                                    Carl Sandburg

93 The Blue Sky—Dana Steichen. Long Island, New York. 1923. Palladium print.
"Who cleaned the sky so clean today? who cleaned my big windows
and opened them to the blue sky? who unfastened the shutters
and the hasps and put this clean blue sky up over?"
                                                      Carl Sandburg

93 The Blue Sky—Dana Steichen. Long Island, New York. 1923. Palladium print.
"Who cleaned the sky so clean today? who cleaned my big windows
and opened them to the blue sky? who unfastened the shutters
and the hasps and put this clean blue sky up over?"
                                                      Carl Sandburg

94 *(below)* "Mr. and Mrs.": The Sandburgs. Elmhurst, Illinois. 1923.

95 *(next page)* Self Portrait with Photographic Paraphernalia. New York. 1929. Photographed for *Vanity Fair*.

I had made several trips to New York during the period from 1920 to 1923, but they were always of short duration. Now I made up my mind that my self-imposed apprenticeship was over. It was time to do something about a career in photography. So, in 1923, I went to New York for a prolonged stay.

On landing in New York, I picked up a copy of *Vanity Fair,* which happened to have a page of portraits of photographers with a wonderful appreciation by Frank Crowninshield, the editor, of the contributions that photographers had made to *Vanity Fair.* My portrait was in the center of the page with the caption, "The greatest living portrait photographer," followed by the statement that, unfortunately, I had given up photography for painting. So I wrote a letter to Crowninshield, thanking him for this gracious tribute to photography, but telling him that his information service was faulty, for I had not given up photography. On the contrary, I had given up painting and decided to devote myself exclusively to photography.

This letter brought a prompt invitation from Crowninshield to meet with him and Condé Nast for lunch. They proposed that I work for the Condé Nast Publications as chief photographer. The work would be largely portraiture of prominent people for *Vanity Fair,* but Crowninshield wondered if I would also be willing to make fashion photographs for *Vogue.* He said they would not use my name with the fashion photographs, if I preferred. My response was that I had already made fashion photographs in 1911, for the magazine *Art et Décoration* (plates 96–99). These were probably the first serious fashion photographs ever made. I also said that, if I made a photograph, I would stand by it with my name; otherwise I wouldn't make it. This pleased Nast, and we agreed in principle on the job.

A few days later, the question of salary came up. When I stated what I thought would be a proper salary, Nast said that it was more than they had ever paid any photographer. I answered, "It was not *my* statement published in *Vanity Fair* that I was the greatest living portrait photographer." So Nast gave in. Although the price we agreed on was higher than they had ever paid, a photographer in the same field today would consider it chicken feed.

Since I did not have a studio of my own, the first portrait sittings I did for *Vanity Fair* were photographed in the studios of the New York Camera Club. The first fashion photographs were made in Nast's apartment. For the first sitting, we had a good-looking young woman wearing a handsome and rather elaborate gown covered down the front with rich embroidery. I had never made photographs with artificial light, but there was the Condé Nast electrician with a battery of about a dozen klieg arcs, wanting to know where he should put the lights. I said, "Just wait," and went to work with the model in the natural daylight of the room. But our good Irish electrician, James McKeon, who later worked entirely for me, kept on asking where I wanted the lights. Finally I realized I would have to do something about it, and I had him bank the lights all in one place and then asked for a couple of bed sheets. No one at a photographic fashion sitting had ever asked for bed sheets, but Carmel Snow, fashion editor of *Vogue* at the time, had a policy that a photographer should have whatever he required, and no questions asked. When the sheets came in, I lined up chairs in front of the electrician's lights and over them draped a four-ply thickness of sheets, so that when he turned on the lights, they didn't interfere with my model. The electrician was satisfied. I heard him say to one of the editors, "That guy knows his stuff." Applied to electric lights, this statement was as far from the truth as anything imaginable.

After that experience I realized that electric light would be my greatest ally in getting variety into fashion pictures. For one whole year, I used daylight plus one light. Then, gradually, I added lights, one at a time, until, in the later years of my work for *Vogue* and *Vanity Fair,* there were lights going all over the place.

A picture editor or art director on a fashion magazine is faced with having to tell the same story year after year. All he has to present are photographs of the newest fashions. To make the pages appear different, he has to secure variety somehow. I had always regarded the layout and presentation of *Vogue* and *Vanity Fair* as namby-pamby, meaningless, and conventional. Happily, not long after I started working for the Condé Nast Publications, Nast brought over from Europe a new art director, Dr. M. F. Agha. Dr. Agha swiftly transformed the layout and picture presentation, and gave both magazines a fresh, live appearance.

When I started making photographs for *Vogue,* I had a great deal to learn about fashion. So I have always felt grateful to Carmel Snow for the real interest she showed in fashion photography and for her invaluable assistance at fashion sittings. She had infinite patience and tact in pointing out to me the essential fashion feature in the pictures we were working on. She also taught me to appreciate the special aptitudes of the different French designers. My favorite in the early days was Vionnet, and Mrs. Snow, recognizing this, always took special delight in bringing me a Vionnet gown to photograph.

My first contribution to the fashion photograph was to make it as realistic as possible. I felt that a woman, when she looked at a picture of a gown, should be able to form a very good idea of how that gown was put together and what it looked like. The group of early fashion pictures in plates 100–103 indicate how I carried out this idea.

After my first year with fashion photographs, a friend of Nast's wrote him a letter which said, "Your Baron de Meyer [my immediate predecessor on the job] made every woman look like a cutie, but Steichen makes even a cutie look like a woman."

I felt that, when a great dressmaker like Vionnet created a gown, it was entitled to a presentation as dignified as the gown itself, and I selected models with that in view.

The greatest fashion model I ever photographed was Marion Morehouse (plates 104 and 107). Miss Morehouse was no more interested in fashion as fashion than I was. But when she put on the clothes that were to be photographed, she transformed herself into a woman who really would wear that gown or that riding habit or whatever the outfit was.

In 1926, I was approached by Ruzzie Green, art director of the Stehli Silk Corporation, with the project of creating a series of photographic designs for silk dress fabrics. I said this would interest me very much if I didn't have to do flowers and garlands. He said, "You can photograph whatever you wish."

I asked, "Would that include lumps of sugar or moth balls, tacks, nails, and so forth?"

He said, "Anything you wish."

So I proceeded to do a series of designs for silk fabrics. One of the best, I thought, was the one of carpet tacks, used as the end papers of this book. This was a very popular design and was one of the first sellouts of the Stehli designs for that year. I also did a design with beans, a checkerboard design with sugar, a polka-dot design with moth balls, and one with spectacles, as well as "The Wandering Thread." The thread was dropped around rather casually on paper and given a dimension by cast shadows. Some of the designs are reproduced in plates 109–112.

96–99 Poiret Fashions. Photographed for *Art et Décoration,* Paris, April, 1911.

100-103 Fashion Photographs for *Vogue*. 1923–1925.

104 Cheruit Gown (Marion Morehouse—Mrs. e. e. cummings). New York. 1927. Photographed for *Vogue*.

105 *Vogue* Fashion: Black. 1934.

106 *Vogue* Fashion: White. 1935.

107 *Vogue* Fashion: Evening Gowns and Wrap. 1930.

108 Nude Torso. 1934. For article—"Vogue Beauty Primer."

Fabric Designs for Stehli Silks:

109 *(preceding page)* Matches and Match Boxes. 1926.

110 *(above)* Spectacles. 1927.

111 *(opposite)* Spectacle Butterfly. 1926.

112 *(next page)* The Wandering Thread. 1927.

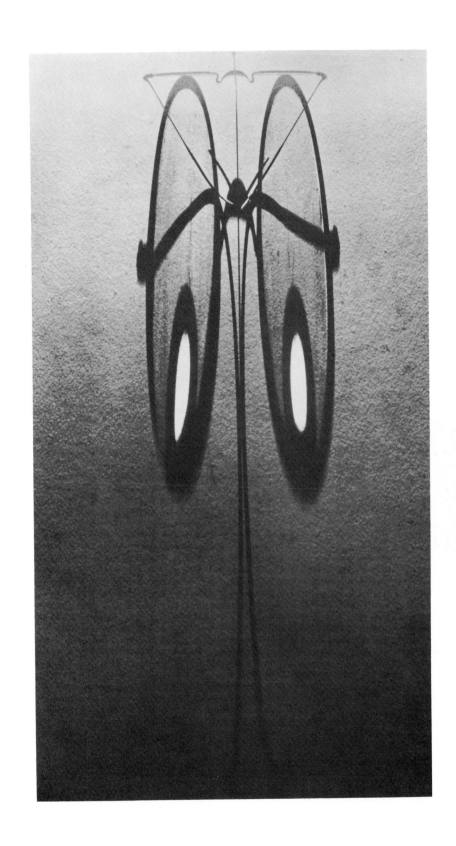

For *Vanity Fair* began a long procession of portraits of the great, the near-great, and the would-be great. It didn't matter whether the sitter was a statesman, a writer, a poet, an actor, a prizefighter, or a musician; they were all interesting. The exciting thing was the variety in this procession that came to my studio to appear on the pages of *Vanity Fair.*

Of course I had favorites. Charlie Chaplin was one. The first time he came to the studio, his secretary, who brought him there, said, "Mr. Chaplin has another appointment, so he can only give you twenty minutes." Then the secretary left. When we got Chaplin in the studio and started to arrange the lights, he froze. I dismissed my assistants and tried to work alone with him, but nothing happened. Finally Chaplin said, "You know, I can't just sit still. I have to be doing something. Then I'm all right."

So I stopped working and got out a portfolio of my photographs, including the Sunflower Series, which interested him very much. He made one remark, "It's curious, the closer you get to nature, the more mysterious it becomes."

Then I started to talk to him about his films, and as I waxed enthusiastic about *The Gold Rush,* the film he had just released, he loosened up and became enthusiastic in turn. I called the men in and in a few minutes I had a half-dozen portraits of Chaplin relaxed and himself, the image of a dancing faun (plate 180).

During the early years on *Vanity Fair,* I made annual trips to Hollywood with one of the editors. It was there that I had a chance to photograph the immortal Greta Garbo. She was working on a picture, *The Green Hat.* I was given a place off the set to use as a photographic studio. The stagehands brought in some gigantic arc lights, which were too much for me. I simply directed them right and left against the ceiling and the walls, so that I would not have to contend with the sharp shadows of crisscross lighting. I watched Garbo at work through a crack in the wall of the set on which she was performing. The director was explaining to her some detail of action that he wanted. It was a simple thing like going up to a table, finding a book, and discovering something in that book. She did it again and again, while the director, not satisfied, continually tried to explain. Finally she said, "I think I'll go away for a while."

Going away meant going off the set and sitting on a chair while her maid put two screens around her. She was in a little box. I don't know what she actually thought, but I visualized her as thinking, "What does that man really want me to do?"

After a while, she came out and said, "All right, let's try it." She rehearsed it once more, and the director said it was fine. After they shot the scene, he said, "Greta, you were wonderful."

Then I was given what I was told would be a five-minute interval in their shooting. In my improvised studio next to the movie set, there was a kitchen chair, and over it I draped a focusing cloth. When Garbo came in to pose for the *Vanity Fair* photograph, I asked her to sit on the chair. She straddled it and used its back for resting her arms. I made five or six exposures, all more or less like her typical movie stills. She moved her head this way and that way, chin up and down, but what bothered me most was her hair. It was curled and fluffy and hung down over her forehead. I said, "It's too bad we're doing this with that movie hairdo."

At that, she put her hands up to her forehead and pushed every strand of hair back away from her face, saying, "Oh, this terrible hair." At that moment, the *woman* came out, like the sun coming out from behind dark clouds. The full beauty of her magnificent face was revealed (plate 125).

After this picture, I suggested we try something else and asked her to stand. As she started to move, her director called out, "Greta, I've given you ten minutes instead of five. We have to go to work."

In reply, she gave him a scowl (plate 124). Then she dashed up to me and put her arms around me saying, "Oh you, you should be motion-picture director. You understand."

And I realized what she meant. I had let her do whatever she wanted, instead of ordering her or asking her to do this or that. I don't think Greta Garbo ever had a chance to make the kind of picture she was really capable of doing. Of course, the real Garbo tragedy is that she stopped working so soon, obsessed with the idea that only a young woman should appear in the movies. Just as she was getting ripe to do really great roles, she stopped. She had done fine things in the movies and was certainly very beautiful, but I do not think she ever came close to fulfilling her potential. Her work was only the beginning of the career she should have had.

The first time I photographed Marlene Dietrich, the job was supervised by Joseph von Sternberg. The Sternberg-Dietrich method of working was a sort of Svengali-Trilby arrangement. She never would pose for anybody unless Sternberg was present, watching her and telling her what to do. That afternoon, I had spent two hours and made about forty exposures, but I was not getting anywhere. Finally, I resorted to pretending I had taken a picture and then trying to steal a shot, for, the moment I was through with a picture, Miss Dietrich relaxed and commenced to talk and was really quite charming. But under Sternberg's gaze, she was about as exciting as a wooden cigar-store Indian.

Sternberg found I was trying to fool them by taking pictures unawares and said, "Oh, you're trying to steal pictures! You don't have to do that with her. Tell her what you want her to do. She can hold it for a week." The day before, when I met him for the first time, he had told me he had directed many of the people I had photographed for *Vanity Fair* and he didn't understand how I got out of them what I did!

At the sitting in which the picture of Marlene Dietrich in plate 140 was made, Sternberg was not present. We had a fine time, and she was her own magical self. When the sitting was over, she said to me in a voice tremulous with excitement, "You know, this is the first time I have ever had a picture made without Sternberg."

Mary Pickford, in being photographed, insisted that there be a floor light in front of her, shooting up into her face. I assume she liked to have the reflection of sparkling lights in her eyes. But the floor light was a very trying handicap for me, and when I dutifully put it on the floor as she requested, I placed a piece of deep-red stage gelatin over it. Since I was using ordinary color-blind plates instead of panchromatic, the gelatin produced the equivalent of no light at all. But Miss Pickford was satisfied, and so was I (plate 129). Later, after I had shown her the pictures, I explained my deception. She was greatly pleased. She told me she had thought the red light would give some special effect, and had been planning to tell the cameraman to use it in her next film.

Some actors seem to become the character they are playing; most actors, on the contrary, always seem to be acting a role. It would be a sacrifice of truth to try to represent one kind of performance as the other kind in a photograph. The picture of John Barrymore as Hamlet (plate 113) is neither a portrait of Barrymore nor a portrait of Hamlet, but a portrait of Barrymore acting the part of Hamlet. To me, the portrait of Nazimova (plate 119) represents the actress who never stops acting, even when she is off stage.

I have photographed Katharine Cornell many times. She is one of our finest actresses but also a remarkable person. I had always photographed her in a part that she knew, and I had often asked her why she did not do any of the Greek dramas. The suggestion seemed so remote to her that it was almost like asking her if she would play God. One day, when we were finished with the regular sitting, I said, "Let's do a Greek tragedy." I draped some cloths around her shoulder and over her head. And I said, "Now you are a woman of ancient Greece, and you are facing the tragedy that fate has in store for you." That was all. Almost at once, she became completely involved in the moment I suggested (plate 114).

The first time I saw Lillian Gish, other than on the movie screen, was as she walked into my studio to be photographed for *Vanity Fair*. As the saying goes, I was knocked for a loop. It was as if an angel had come into the place. Every movement she made and everything she said seemed full of magic. I made pictures fast and wildly and believed they were all wonderful. But that night, when I looked at the negatives, even before seeing the proofs, I realized I didn't have anything at all. I had allowed my emotional reaction to take charge of that sitting and had lost all charge of myself. This was a valuable lesson, but a very embarrassing one, for I had to go to Miss Gish with the proofs and beg her to come and sit again for me. She was very gracious about my chagrin. When she came again, I decided to do a fanciful version of *Romola,* a romantic role she was planning to undertake. I put flowers in her hair and then let her own sweetness and youngness take over (plate 116).

Quite a few years later, on the edge of my pond in the country, I did some studies of Lillian Gish as Ophelia. We had talked about the moment, described in *Hamlet,* when Ophelia "fell in the weeping brook" and drowned.

I had thought a lot about producing the quality of Ophelia's madness, and one of the things I had prepared was some infrared film and an infrared filter. I knew this would turn Miss Gish's eyes into dark spots and help give a wild look. But the success of the picture lay in Miss Gish's performance. From the moment she stepped to the edge of the pond and grasped the trailing branch of the willow tree, she was no longer Lillian Gish. She had become Ophelia, "a document in madness" (plate 117).

The Charlie Chaplin pictures (plate 126) were made the second time I photographed him. I remembered how, at his first sitting, we had had difficulty breaking through his avowed self-consciousness. He had said, "I have to be doing something." So I planned to do a sequence of pictures. When Chaplin arrived that afternoon, he was in a chipper, gay, and dancing mood. I took him into the studio and pointed to two white panels, one set vertically and the other as a horizontal seat. "Your set," I said, then indicated that he should sit on the far end of the horizontal panel. After the camera was focused and ready to shoot, I placed his hat on the near end of the panel without a word of explanation. Chaplin was obviously puzzled. I made the first exposure. Then, while the film was being changed, I moved the hat a little closer to him. He smiled and moved his cane. After that picture was made, I moved the hat still closer to him. He raised his cane as if it were a gun. For the next picture, I jerked the hat away. His posture relaxed, and he smiled a congenial, victory smile. The four pictures were assembled into a montage.

Working for the same magazine, year in, year out, when I was frequently assigned to cover actors and actresses in portraits or in plays, I was sometimes hard put to it to find a new situation. For this reason, even in doing a portrait of a character in a play, I always sought to create some kind of improvisation. In the case of W. C. Fields, there was nothing in his act that suggested the scene in plate 143. I simply set up a kind of tenement back yard with a poster on a wall and laundry hanging out and trash lying all around. And Fields came out of the dressing room in his pajamas. He spied a cake of ice in a pan near the set. He lifted up the cake of ice and walked into the set, and we made the picture. That was all.

The day I made the picture in plate 128, Gloria Swanson and I had had a long session, with many changes of costume and different lighting effects. At the end of the session, I took a piece of black lace veil and hung it in front of her face. She recognized the idea at once. Her eyes dilated, and her look was that of a leopardess lurking behind leafy shrubbery, watching her prey. You don't have to explain things to a dynamic and intelligent personality like Miss Swanson. Her mind works swiftly and intuitively.

In photographing Beatrice Lillie, I discovered that she does everything for the photographer; all he has to do is press the button. I would have had a hard job spoiling her wonderful spoof on "Rule, Britannia," plate 141.

Martha Graham comes up with ideas so fast it's hard to keep pace. She understood that I couldn't photograph her while she was dancing, because fast film had not yet been developed, so she moved into sculptural gestures and held them for an instant. Each movement was related to the preceding movement or to the next one. In the photograph made just before the one in the right-hand side of plate 118, her arm and hair were held straight up. Then came a downward action, which she balanced with her other arm, producing a horizontal movement. After this, the arm dropped, and she pulled part of her drapery high up over her head. She produced a combination of dancing, choreography, and heroic sculpture.

In plates 145–152 are a group of improvisations related to specific plays. But none of them is an actual scene from a play. For instance, when I photographed the three corporals from *What Price Glory?*, I found out that each of the three boys had been in the war, just as I had, so we enacted a number of real-life scenes we remembered. One was looking for cooties (plate 145).

The three characters from the play *Ethan Frome* had only a couple of boards to work with. They used them to give the impression of eavesdropping, which Pauline Lord, with her inimitable genius, made very live (plate 150).

When the wonderful cast of Negro actors from *The Green Pastures* came to my studio, I made individual portraits of them and then prepared to do the entire group in the march to the Promised Land. To avoid the straight line that occurred on the stage, I arranged the group in different levels. The spread (plate 155) was made in two separate pictures joined together. Some of the actors appear in both shots. The troupe performed for me like veterans, and they also gave me the pleasure of their singing throughout the entire sitting; the singing contributed a certain reality to the picture.

When I photographed George Arliss, he was playing Disraeli in the play *Old English*. When I announced that the sitting was over, and he started to walk away, I had him stop once more and got the picture in plate 156. This rear view may not have pleased him, but it was greatly appreciated by my editors.

113 *(preceding page)* John Barrymore as Hamlet. New York. 1922.
114 *(above)* Katharine Cornell—Improvisation. New York. 1934.

115 Katharine Cornell in "The Barretts of Wimpole Street." New York. 1931.

116 *(above)* Lillian Gish as "Romola." New York. 1923.

117 *(opposite)* Lillian Gish as Ophelia. Connecticut. 1936.

118 *(above)* Martha Graham. New York. 1931.

119 *(opposite)* Nazimova. New York. 1931.

120 *(opposite)* Paul Robeson as "The Emperor Jones." New York. 1933.

121 *(above)* Paul Muni in "Key Largo." New York. 1940.

122 Maurice Chevalier Does a Song and Dance. New York. 1929.

123 Fred Astaire—Top Hat in "Funny Face." New York. 1927.

126 Charlie Chaplin. New York. 1931.

127 *(opposite)* Anna May Wong. New York. 1930.
128 *(above)* Gloria Swanson. New York. 1924.

129 Mary Pickford. Hollywood. 1927.

130 Sylvia Sidney. Hollywood. 1931.

131 *(left)* La Argentina. Paris. 1928.

132 *(right)* Escudero. Paris. 1932.

133 *(left)*   Jimmy Savo. New York. 1929.

134 *(right)* Ann Pennington. New York. 1925.

135 Eugene O'Neill and George M. Cohan—"Ah, Wilderness!" New York. 1933. Negative montage.

136 *(opposite)* Improvisation—"Strange Interlude," with Lynn Fontanne. New York. 1928. Negative montage.

137 *(above)* Lupe Velez and Conrad Veidt. Hollywood. 1929. Detail of a multiple exposure.

138 *(opposite)* Frederic March and Miriam Hopkins in "Dr. Jekyll and Mr. Hyde." Hollywood. 1931. Multiple exposure.

139 Erich von Stroheim. Hollywood. 1927.

140 Marlene Dietrich. New York. 1932.

143 *(opposite)* W. C. Fields. New York. 1925.

144 *(above)*   Ed Wynn. New York. 1930.

145 Improvisation—"What Price Glory?"

New York. 1924.

146 Improvisation—"Processional."

New York. 1925.

147 Improvisation—"Burlesque"

—Barbara Stanwyck and Hal Skelly. New York. 1928.

148 Jimmy Durante (center).

Clayton, Jackson, and Durante. New York. 1929.

149 Improvisation—"The Barker"—Walter Huston. New York. 1927.

150 Improvisation—"Ethan Frome"—Ruth Gordon, Raymond Massey, and Pauline Lord. New York. 1936.

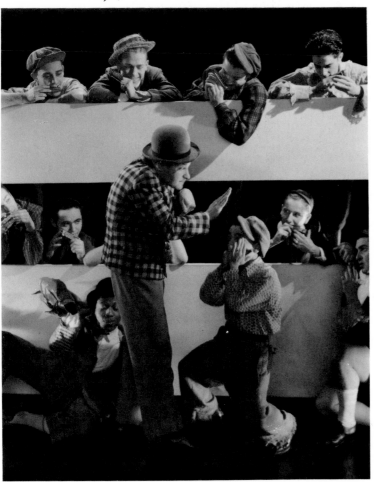

151 Borah Minevitch and his "Harmonica Rascals." New York. 1931.

152 Improvisation—"The Front Page" —Osgood Perkins and Lee Tracy. New York. 1928.

153 *(opposite)* Gerhardt Hauptmann. New York. 1932.

154 *(above)* Wesley Hill as Gabriel in "The Green Pastures." New York. 1930.

155 *(next pages)* "The Green Pastures." Exodus to the Promised Land. New York. 1930.

Not long after I began working for *Vogue* and *Vanity Fair,* I was approached by the J. Walter Thompson agency and asked if I would be interested in doing some advertising work. I had been watching the magazines and was distressed by how little and how badly photography was being used. So, when the agency proposed an interesting idea for Jergens Lotion, I took the job.

The idea was to photograph the hands of a woman who did her own housework. Among the situations suggested, I liked particularly that of peeling potatoes.

Mrs. Stanley Resor, wife of the president of J. Walter Thompson, posed for the hands, and I could tell by the way she cut the potatoes that this wasn't the first time she had done it. The picture (plate 157) is shown the way I had wanted it reproduced, that is, cropped in close, but the advertiser decided on using the entire negative, which showed more of the bowl of potatoes and more of the woman's hands and arms.

Several years later, I received a commission to do an advertising campaign for the Eastman Kodak Company. This again appealed to me because of the realism involved. The campaign, which ran for several years, was based on people looking at snapshots. I decided not to use professional models. The agency was to find everyday people in the suburbs and various towns around New York. The result was that one of the staff did a piece of casting the like of which Hollywood has never been able to achieve. To make each picture as real as possible, I worked out a specific procedure. First, I set up the composition in a general way, with the people looking at some nondescript snapshots. But I had in reserve a selection from the Eastman Kodak files of lively snapshots of subjects that would particularly interest the people I was photographing. Just as I got ready to make the exposure, I handed this set of snapshots to them. In every case, they were greatly interested and their expressions were spontaneous and real (plates 160 and 161).

In addition to doing commercial advertising for firms, J. Walter Thompson did a number of promotions for organizations and charities. "On the Clinic Stairs" (plate 158) was done for the Manhattan Eye, Ear and Throat Hospital.

"Death Takes a Holiday" (plate 159) was made for the New York Post-Graduate Hospital.

Then there was the story of the homeless women in New York lodging houses during the Depression. It seemed that many women, old and young, jobless or too old to work and contribute to the family food supply, left home and came to New York. When the Travelers Aid Society found such people, they put them up in lodging houses for the night. We were to do a brochure for the Travelers Aid Society, and I suggested that the agency bring up the first twenty women who came out of the lodging house in the morning. There was to be no selecting. Each woman was to be given ten dollars.

To make a composition that was both vertical and horizontal for a double-page spread, I had tables, chairs, and stepladders prepared. When the women arrived, they were placed in groups that made an over-all pattern on the two pages. I placed the older women in the foreground as the focal point in the composition. To get the rudderless feeling of their story, I instructed each woman to look in a different direction.

At first, when the women came into the studio, every one of them, even the grandmothers, started to primp. But very soon, they forgot all about me and the cameras and the studio. Their attention reverted to their own problems (plate 162). It was a heartbreaking experience to see these lovely people in such a hopeless situation, especially since the group included so many ages and stages—the little child and the aged, white-faced woman whose glazed eyes seemed to be staring at death, the young women with the hard, resentful faces, and the innocent teen-ager who had been found by the Travelers Aid Society wandering aimlessly about Grand Central Station. The picture opposite plate 162 is an enlarged detail.

The photograph "Homeless Women" as a composition presented the same problem that painters of all periods have had in making large groups. Painters didn't have the difficulty of posing all the models in a group at one time, but the basic problem of making a coherent whole was the same.

I also made a series of pictures for the Federation of Jewish Philanthropies that were to be used for a booklet soliciting financial help. This job came at a time when we

156 *(opposite)* George Arliss in "Old English." New York. 1924.

were getting the news of Hitler's early humiliation of the Jews; they were made to wear arm bands, their stores were labeled, their windows were smashed. I wanted one picture as a sort of answer to this. I asked for a white-haired, strongly built woman and a huge Bible. She was brought to the studio dressed just as I photographed her in "The Matriarch" (plate 164). She couldn't understand my language, and I couldn't understand hers, so my communication with her was all in sign language; but she seemed to grasp it. I hoped that the whole composition would have a certain majesty and, above all, the strength of something invincible.

157 Peeling Potatoes. Advertisement for Jergens Lotion. 1923.
The Andrew Jergens Company. J. Walter Thompson Agency.

158 *(opposite)* On the Clinic Stairs. Publicity for Manhattan Eye, Ear and Throat Hospital. 1931.
J. Walter Thompson Agency.

159 *(below)* "Death Takes a Holiday." Dr. John F. Erdmann operating. Publicity for New York Post-Graduate Hospital. 1929.
J. Walter Thompson Agency.

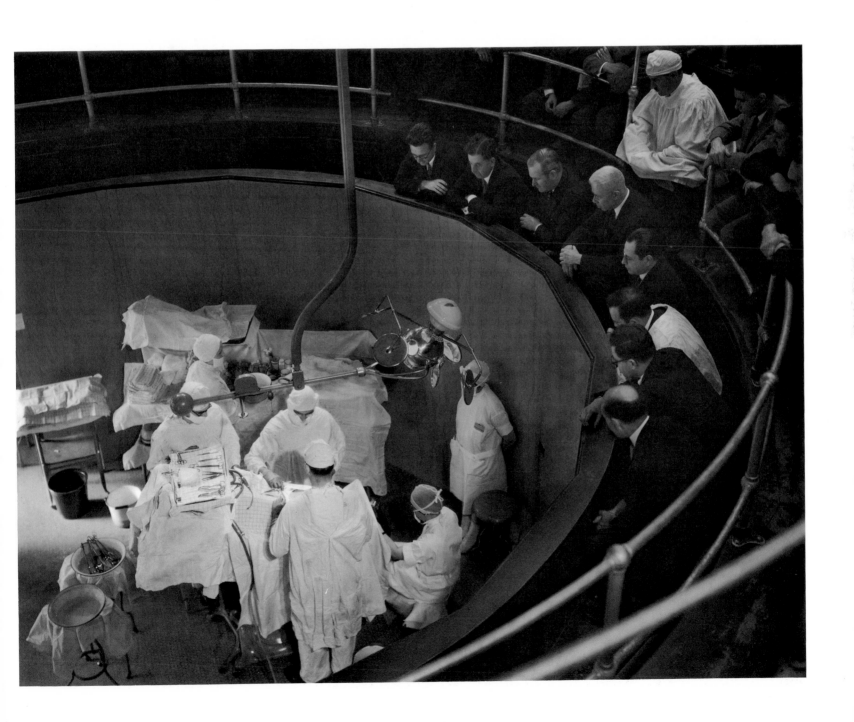

160 Advertisement for Eastman Kodak Company "Snapshots." 1933. J. Walter Thompson Agency.

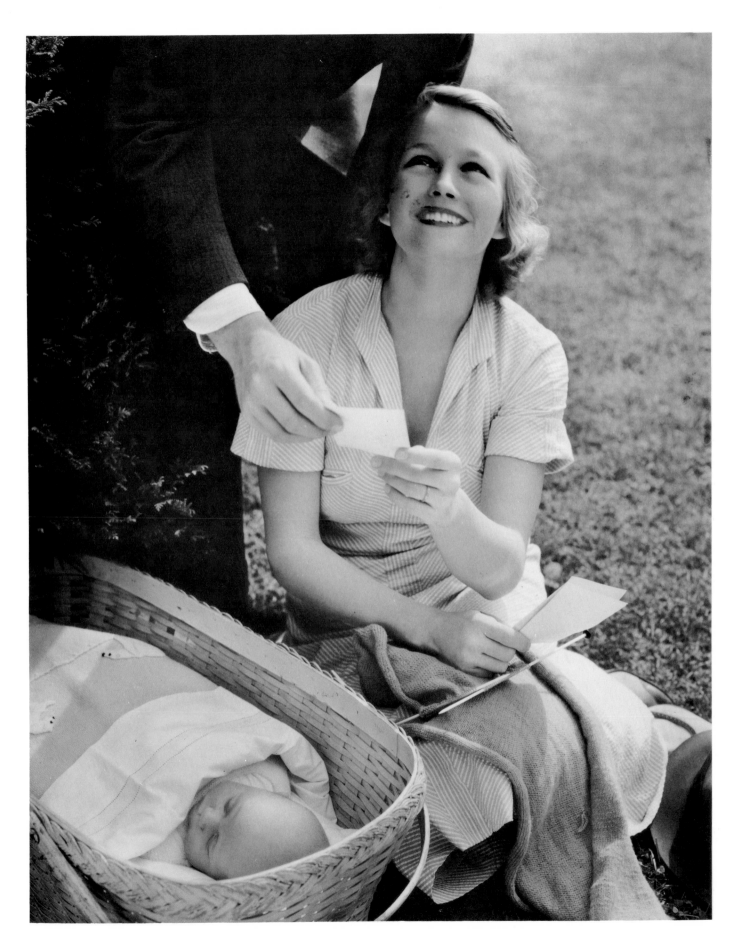

161 Advertisement for Eastman Kodak Company "Snapshots." 1933. J. Walter Thompson Agency.

162 *(opposite)* Homeless Women: The Depression. Publicity for Travelers Aid Society. 1932. J. Walter Thompson Agency.

163 *(below)* Homeless Women: The Depression. (Detail.) 1932. J. Walter Thompson Agency.

164 *(next page)* The Matriarch. For Federation of Jewish Philanthropies of New York. 1935. J. Walter Thompson Agency.

The artist, in any medium, does not live in a vacuum. There is a relationship between everything that is being done and everything that has been done before. The modern artist is in step not only with the general cultural aspects of his time but also with the specific scientific aspects of research, invention, and discovery. And the artist's understanding and appreciation is often far ahead of that part of the public which clings desperately to the things that have gone before.

The history of painting probably began in the caves as much as ten thousand years ago. The history of photography, the process of fixing an image produced by the aid of light, began about a hundred and twenty years ago. In spite of this vast difference in age, photography and painting have had a great deal of influence on each other. This influence is certainly not harmful, except when it leads, in either case, to the imitation of techniques or to the still more serious imitation of basic concepts suitable only to one medium. Then it becomes a blind alley.

The painter who consciously took the first great step toward the complete elimination of the literal representation of objects in modern art was Paul Cézanne. By coincidence, Cézanne was born the same year that the daguerreotype process was presented to the world. Today, certainly, the modern abstract painter has dumped the business of literal representation lock, stock, and barrel into the lap of the photographer. In the process, certain venerable traditions, such as portrait painting, have, like the horse-drawn vehicle, all but disappeared.

The camera is a witness of objects, places, and events. A photograph of an object is, in a sense, a portrait. But the camera with its glass eye, the lens, and its memory, the film, can in itself produce little more than mirrored verisimilitudes. A good photograph requires more than that. When an artist of any kind looks at his subject, he looks with everything he is. Everything that he has lived, learned, observed, and experienced combines to enable him to identify himself with the subject and look with insight, perception, imagination, and understanding. The technical process simply serves as a vehicle of transcription and not as the art.

It takes a powerful generative force to produce a work of art in any medium. This force may be sparked by a spontaneous happening intuitively perceived, but to become valid as truth, the intuition must be tested by intellectual processes of verification. The photographer, unlike the painter and regardless of his subjective feelings, is forced by the very nature of his medium to concentrate on the object, on what Goethe referred to as *"Das Ding an sich"* in a portrait: on the person, or the meadow, the mountain, the flowers, or the horse being photographed.

Photography is a medium of formidable contradictions. It is both ridiculously easy and almost impossibly difficult. It is easy because its technical rudiments can readily be mastered by anyone with a few simple instructions. It is difficult because, while the artist working in any other medium begins with a blank surface and gradually brings his conception into being, the photographer is the only imagemaker who begins with the picture completed. His emotions, his knowledge, and his native talent are brought into focus and fixed beyond recall the moment the shutter of his camera has closed.

It has sometimes been said of the work of certain portrait painters that, by prolonged study and work with the model, they were able to produce a synthesis of the sitter's complete personality. But here we must remember that it took great writers like Balzac or Proust volumes to bring us a living portrait of a person. To imagine that a visual artist in any medium could condense a complete portrait into one picture is putting a strain on logic. Every human being has the capacity for both laughter and tears, and there is no point halfway between that combines the infinite range of human complexities and contradictory states of heart and mind involved in the human condition. However, the vocabulary of photography offers greater potential for the making of complete portraits than any other visual art. The simplicity and swiftness of the photographic process permits an almost limitless number of photographs to be made reflecting endless sequences of moods and conditions.

Leonardo da Vinci is reputed to have spent two years painting the portrait of Mona Lisa, and the picture is said to be of an enigmatic woman with a baffling smile. Alfred Stieglitz worked twenty-seven years to produce an extensive series of photographs of his wife, Georgia O'Keeffe. Within the space of any two of those years, he made hundreds of photographs of the different moods and moments expressed by her face, and to these he added a unique series of expressive photographs of her neck, feet, hands, and torso. This entire series is certainly the most comprehensive and intimate portrayal of a single person that has ever been realized by any of the visual arts.

During the thirteen years of my own portrait activities for *Vanity Fair,* although the accent was on the performing arts, the almost daily procession in portraiture also brought in distinguished persons in many fields. The subjects to be photographed were selected and sent to me by the editors of *Vanity Fair.* Usually, these subjects were in the public eye at the moment, for one reason or another. So, in a sense, the portraits I made of them belonged to the field of photo-journalism.

Most of the time, I had never seen these people until they walked into the studio, and, in some cases, I knew little or nothing about them. But some were sent to me several times over the years. One of the most welcome of the "repeaters" was Eugene O'Neill. His coming to the studio was always a red-letter day and when he arrived, the whole place became electrified, not only by his presence but also by the very high esteem in which I held his work. My admiration had really begun with his father, for the elder O'Neill's *Monte Cristo* was one of the first plays I had seen as a boy. The name O'Neill had been for a long time directly and vividly associated in my mind with the theater. The playwright was a unique sitter in another respect. He never reflected any consciousness of the camera. He was always O'Neill.

The last sitting I did of him was at my request. This time, when I photographed him, I tried to imagine him on the stage working with the actors in one of his plays, so I used stage lighting, more or less, for the large head in plate 182. At the time of this sitting, I also photographed his beautiful wife, the former Carlotta Monterey (plate 181).

There are a number of portraits which I did not originally make for *Vanity Fair* but which were subsequently used in the magazine. One of these is the multiple heads of Carl Sandburg (plate 166). I photographed Carl on the day after he had corrected the last proof sheet of his biography of Lincoln, *The War Years,* on which he had been working for uncounted years of research and six years of writing. Carl sat at the breakfast table that morning with

a serene and relaxed look, a look that brought to mind Gardner's beautiful photographs of Lincoln made the day after the Civil War surrender. This is the only picture of Lincoln in existence which shows a real smile, a tired smile of relief, a smile of infinite warmth and tenderness.

The photograph of the life mask of Abraham Lincoln (plate 167) is a photograph that I look upon with a real sense of achievement. One of the early casts of the mask was in the collection of Frederick Meserve, and he loaned it to me for several months while I studied it under all possible conditions. I felt that this mask was more than an authentic document. It must contain something of the inner man, even if that something is only discomfort, for the casting of such a mask from the living face is not a pleasant ordeal. The gouges where the eyes had been covered during the making of the mask were empty dark sockets, so the mask seemed to be the skull of Lincoln with a covering of living flesh. After several months of study and experiment, I found the light that brought out the lines reflecting a feeling of concern. The photograph of the mask revealed an expression which must have been characteristic of Lincoln but which was never shown in any other portrait. I take great satisfaction in what Oliver R. Barrett, the great Lincoln collector, said of this photograph: "The photograph brings out more than the physical mask. The beholder may return to it many times across the years and find its silence sacred and moving. It is a masterpiece of Lincoln portraiture, a supreme interpretation."

I did not have the mask of Goethe, but used an existing photograph of it combined with the spiral shell to suggest the universal qualities of his genius (plate 165).

The portraits of Brancusi (plates 176 and 177) bring up vivid memories of a long and warm friendship. Our acquaintance began with a casual meeting at Rodin's studio in Meudon. Some time later, in 1909 or 1910, I saw his statue of "L'Oiseau d'Or," since renamed "Maiastra," exhibited in the Salon des Indépendants. It appealed to me immediately as the most wonderful concept and execution I had seen by any sculptor with the exception of Rodin. Although my means were scarcely those of an art collector, I wanted this statue so much that I inquired the price at the desk of the exhibition secretary. I was told one thousand francs (two hundred dollars). This was more than I could possibly pay, but, after studying our resources and our budget, I did figure that, by a little squeezing and cutting here and there, I could manage five hundred francs. So I asked for Brancusi's address and went to see him. When I arrived and asked the concierge for Brancusi, she stepped into the courtyard and, putting her hands to her mouth, shouted, "Monsieur Brancusi!" A bearded head appeared at a window and I recognized the man I had met at Rodin's. We greeted each other almost like old friends. I told him my story, and he decided that, if "L'Oiseau d'Or" didn't sell during the exhibition, he didn't see any reason why he shouldn't sell it to a "confrère" for five hundred francs.

It did not sell at the exhibition, so I acquired the bird and moved it out to our home in Voulangis. When Brancusi expressed interest in my idea of placing the sculpture in the garden, we invited him out to visit. At a lumber yard, he found a square piece of wood about ten feet long and made a separate base that harmonized with the short stone pillar on which the bird rested. "L'Oiseau d'Or" reigned over a garden of flower beds.

One day I overheard my six-year-old daughter, Mary, discussing the statue with Brancusi. Mary argued that the position of the bird's head was impossible. No bird could sing with the head in a horizontal position. A bird sang with the head pointed skyward. Brancusi tried to explain that this bird wasn't singing; it was a mythological bird that, according to legend, guided a Roumanian prince through life, and it was talking. But Mary was adamant in her argument. I do not know whether this discussion had any conscious or subconscious effect on Brancusi, but, later, he commenced to make other versions of the bird in which the head was gradually lifted and straightened. In the final version, arrived at in 1935, not only was the movement sharply upward, but the abstract suggestion of an open mouth was also made by an abrupt, bias-cut angle at the top. (This final version was named "Bird in Space" by Brancusi and not "Bird in Flight" as it is often translated.)

When I saw it first, it had just come from the foundry as a crude mass of bronze. But even in the rough state, it seemed a supreme achievement, and I told Brancusi I would like the privilege of having an option on buying it when it was finished. I saw it in its finished state a year later, when he also had a large marble version under way. (The marble version was purchased by Mr. and Mrs. Eugene Meyer.)

When I brought my "Bird in Space" back to America, it was held up in the Customs House and refused duty-free entry as a work of art. It was finally admitted under the classification of Kitchen Utensils and Hospital Supplies, and I was made to pay some six hundred dollars duty on it. I resented the Customs House decision very much and determined to appeal it. One day I mentioned this at a party in the presence of Mrs. Harry Payne Whitney, whose efforts on behalf of modern art led to the founding of The Whitney Museum of American Art. Mrs. Whitney immediately said that this case could establish an important precedent. She asked if I would let her and her lawyers take it over under the heading of "Brancusi vs. the United States." I was grateful for this offer and accepted it.

When the case came up for trial, important museum directors, art critics, and artists testified in favor of Brancusi. The judges finally decided that it wasn't in the province of Uncle Sam to act as an authority in defining a work of art, but that the United States would have to accept the opinion of competent, recognized art authorities. Apparently, our witnesses had established such competence, and the "Bird in Space" won out for Brancusi.

Because the press had accorded this case all the attention of a scandal, Brancusi always referred to it as the "brouhaha." One winter, I made a series of photographs of the bird in my home in Connecticut. I photographed it on the diagonal, with the late afternoon sun playing tricks of light, shade and sparkle with the bronze. I called this series "Brouhaha" (plates 178 and 179).

164a *(left)* Rachmaninoff. New York. 1936. Made for *Life* magazine. Dye transfer print.
165 *(opposite)* Mask of Goethe and Spiral. 1932.

166 *(above)* Carl Sandburg. Connecticut. 1936. Montage.

167 *(opposite)* Life Mask of Abraham Lincoln by Leonard W. Volk, Chicago, March, 1860; photographed 1935.

168 *(above)* Winston Churchill. New York. 1932.

169 *(opposite)* Franklin Delano Roosevelt, then Governor of New York. New York. 1929.

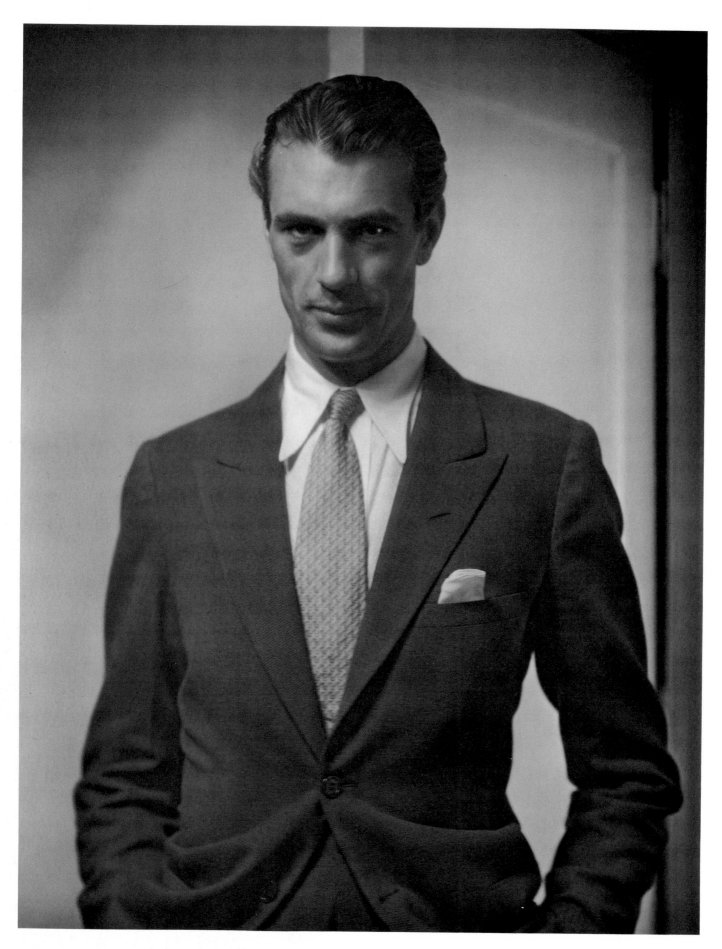

170 *(above)* Gary Cooper. Hollywood. 1930.

171 *(opposite)* Gallant Fox. Long Island. 1930.

172 *(opposite)* Thomas Mann. New York. 1934.
173 *(below)* Elisabeth Bergner in "Escape Me Never." New York. 1935.

176 Brancusi. Voulangis, France. c. 1922.

177 *(opposite)* Brancusi in his Studio. Paris. 1927.

178-179 Brouhaha. Brancusi versus the U.S.
(Photographs 1957-58.)

180 Charlie Chaplin. New York. 1925.

181 *(above)* Carlotta Monterey (Mrs. Eugene O'Neill). New York. 1932.
182 *(opposite)* Eugene O'Neill. New York. 1932.

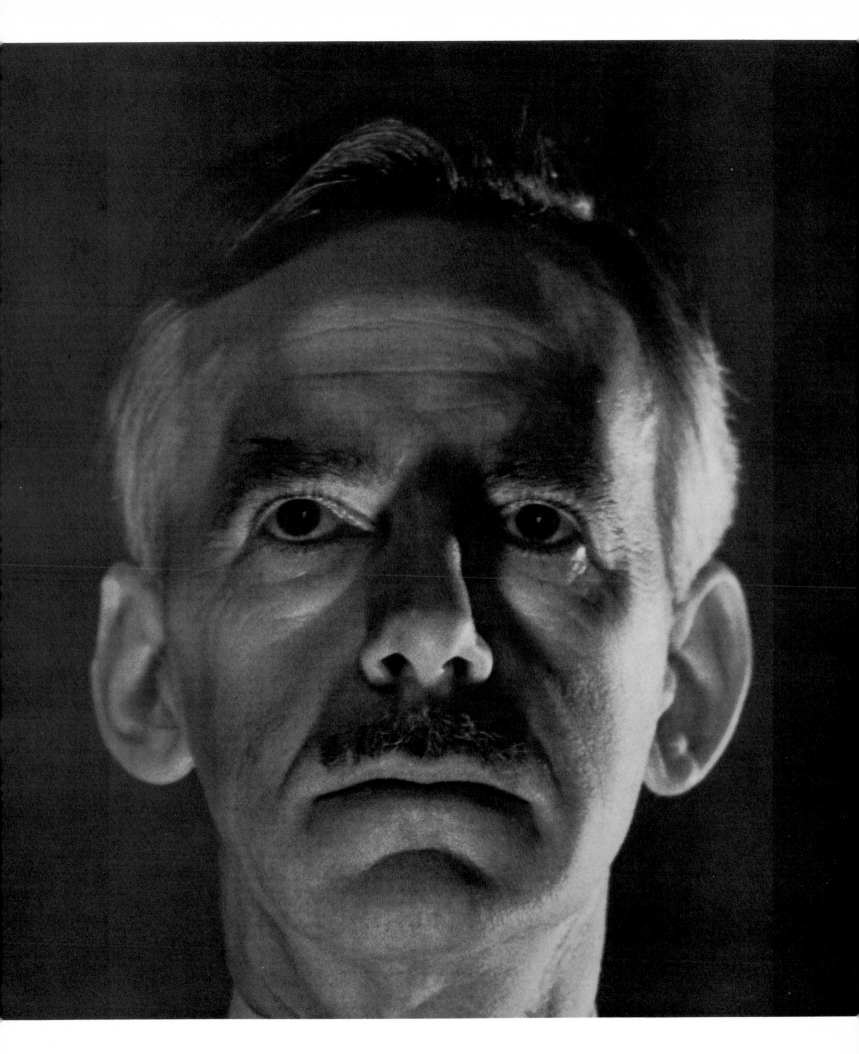

183 H. G. Wells. New York. 1931.

184 Eugene Meyer. New York. 1932.

185 Sinclair Lewis. New York. 1932.

186 Willa Cather. New York. 1926.

187 Bernard M. Baruch. New York. 1932.

188 Henry R. Luce. New York. 1935.

189 Charles Laughton. New York. 1935.

190 Joan Crawford. New York. 1932.

191 Alexander Woollcott. New York. 1933.

192 H. L. Mencken. New York. 1926.

193 *(below)* George M. Cohan. New York. 1933.

194 *(opposite)* Heywood Broun. New York. 1930.

203 Robert Moses. New York. 1935.

204 Jacob Epstein. New York. 1927.

207 Sunburn. New York. 1925.

208 Alexander de Salzman. New York. 1932.

Throughout the period of my commercial photography in advertising and journalism, I kept other active interests going. There was, first of all, my delphinium breeding, which is still a vital preoccupation today. Also I made photographs of things that had little or nothing to do with the work I was doing professionally. These "extra-curricular" photographs were the stimulus that really kept me on the alert and going.

I often photographed things that I saw from the windows of my studio in the Beaux Arts Building on Fortieth Street. A few are reproduced here: "Stars on Sixth Avenue" (plate 210), "Drizzle on 40th Street" (plate 211), and "Sunday Night on 40th Street" (plate 212). I also took my camera around New York and tried to express the significance of the skyscrapers and the bridges. The Empire State Building remained a challenge until I conceived of the building as a Maypole and made the double exposure to suggest the swirl of a Maypole dance (plate 213). I made the pictures of Rockefeller Center (plate 214) into a montage to include the several units and represent the workmen as symbols of the builders. The George Washington Bridge (plate 216) was the first photograph I ever exhibited at The Museum of Modern Art in New York. I also made the illustrations for a Limited Editions Club edition of Thoreau's *Walden*. This project necessitated trips to Walden Pond at different seasons over a period of two years. One of these illustrations is reproduced as plate 215.

In 1930, my daughter Mary, now grownup and married, came to me with a proposition. She said she felt the need of some kind of book to interest her small children in pictures, and she had an idea for a book to be called *The First Picture Book—Everyday Things for Babies*. I found the idea intriguing, so Mary and I produced it together. I made realistic still-life photographs of the objects that a small child could recognize as part of his life. One was a picture of a washstand with a toothbrush set in a glass. After the book was published, a letter came from a mother telling us that, when her child came to this picture, he stopped, made the gesture of taking the brush out of the glass, and then simulated the movement of brushing his teeth. He ended the performance by spitting into the washbasin in the picture! A reproduction from *The First Picture Book—Everyday Things for Babies* appears in plate 209.

In 1929, I acquired a farm in Redding, Connecticut. From the weekends and holidays spent there, came a stream of photographs that were a vital expression of the earth. Three of these appear as plates 217, 218, and 219. The photograph of the dead chestnut branch (plate 217) is a reminder of one of the great tragedies of nature. The chestnut, one of America's most beautiful and valuable trees, was completely wiped out by a fungus disease. When I first moved to Redding, I saw the gaunt skeletons of the chestnut trees all over the countryside.

The photographs I made in the country, as well as the crossbreeding and growing of delphinium and other flowering plants, kept me in contact with nature and kept my hands in contact with the soil. Without this sustenance, I don't believe I could have remained alive and interested in my professional photographic activities in New York for as long as I did.

In 1938, I decided to close my New York studio. The work was not stimulating any more. There was no longer the excitement of new problems to be solved. There was too much repetition and practically no experimentation. Fashion photography had become a routine, and routines are stifling. I found the advertising becoming more and more artificial, and I disliked some of the approaches to it that were developing. Among these were the sex appeal approaches designed to sell lotions or cosmetics or hair preparations by implying that a girl stood no chance of finding a mate unless she used these products. But the real fault was my own. I had lost interest because I no longer found the work challenging; it was too easy. In 1937, I had received an award for distinguished service to advertising, but now I was no longer contributing such a service.

I was not closing my studio because I wanted to retire. After all, I was only fifty-nine. I simply wanted once more to give myself a revitalizing change and move into new areas.

First, I planned to take a long-delayed and much needed vacation. For a long time, I had been envying some of my friends their use of the small 35-mm camera. I had been using the big, clumsy 8 × 10 studio camera. The mobility possible with the 35-mm camera appealed to me as opening a new phase of photography. So the Carl Zeiss Company in New York fitted me out with a Contax and the various lenses I needed, including a round-the-corner finder that permitted making pictures of people when they were not aware that they were being photographed. Plate 222 shows a result of this technique. I put in a good supply of Koda-chrome film, and Dana and I started off for a two months' vacation in Mexico. There, everything was dazzling, exciting, and new, and the Mexican sunlight was a real challenge to color film.

The introduction of Kodachrome color film at last made the use of color available to the art of photography as a practical technique. At first it became more of a liability than an asset, for it brought forth an orgy of color. Instead of colorful pictures we had coloriferous images.

Color photography can be considered as a technique that enriches the value of a photograph as visual information and documentation, but in the domain of abstract photography I believe it can be regarded as an entirely new medium. I devoted much time to experimenting with it as a new medium, but without coming to a conclusive or convincing solution, and I believe that today, in the field of abstract images, there is a richly rewarding opportunity for exploration.

My first real contact with the Indians was at Patzcuaro. These were the Tarascan Indians, of whom I was told they were the only Indians in Mexico who had never been conquered by the Spaniards. Further south, on the Isthmus of Tehuantepec, was the land of the beautiful, stately Tehuana women. But most intriguing of all was Yucatan with its fabulous ruins and its record of the Mayan Indian civilization. The faces of the charming and gentle twentieth-century Mayans (plate 220) were duplicates of the frescoes and carvings of their ancestors.

The relics of the ancient Mayan civilization in Yucatan brought to my sensibilities a new realm of understanding. The art of the ancient Mayans was excellent. They had reached a state of curious and remarkable sophistication in design. Among other achievements, they had developed an advanced knowledge of astronomy. They were curiously inept, however, at invention. They did not solve the problem of the arch, nor did they discover the wheel and its uses. To grow food, they cut down the jungle and planted their seed in the rich, age-old compost of the tropical jungle floor. When they exhausted the soil in a given area, they moved to another one and started the process over again. Archaeologists told me that, when the distance between the cities and the farms became too great, they abandoned the old cities and built new ones closer to the farms.

All told, as I look back at my experience in Yucatan, I still feel curiosity and nostalgia. It is one place in which I have spent a little time that has left me with a strong desire to return.

210 Stars on Sixth Avenue. New York. 1925.

211 *(above)* Drizzle on 40th Street. New York. 1925.

212 *(opposite)* Sunday Night on 40th Street. New York. 1925.

216 *(preceding page)* George Washington Bridge. New York. 1931.

217 *(above)* Dead Chestnut Branch. Connecticut. 1930.

218 *(opposite)* Venerable Tree Trunk. Connecticut. 1932.

219 *(next page)* Singing Wires and Buzzing Bees. Connecticut. 1932.

220 Yucatan: Mayan Women. 1938. Dye transfer print from 35 mm. Kodachrome.

221 Yucatan: The Man Child. 1938.

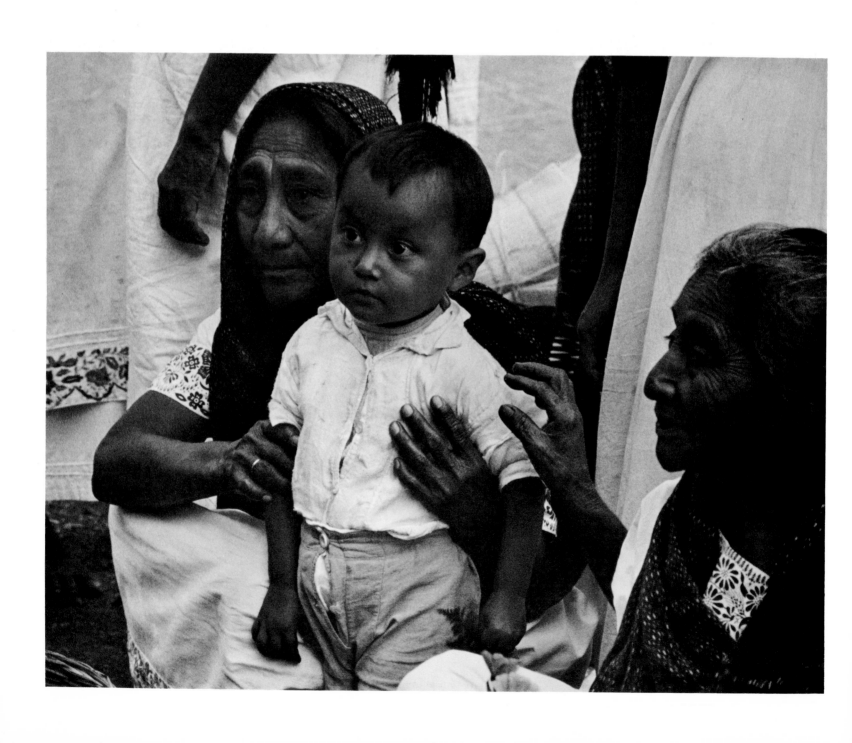

222 Mexico: Market at Patzcuaro. 1938. Dye transfer print from 35 mm. Kodachrome.

Most of the world realized too late in the 1930s that Hitler's unchecked progress was leading to another war. All of Hitler's actions—his inflammatory rantings, his humiliating persecution of the Jews followed by his barbaric project for their extermination, his paralyzing invasions of nations after ruthless bombing attacks—all these things piled up and accelerated until finally no one could fail to see that World War II was inevitable.

My own feelings of revulsion toward war had not diminished since 1917. But, in the intervening years, I had gradually come to believe that, if a real image of war could be photographed and presented to the world, it might make a contribution toward ending the specter of war. This idea made me eager to participate in creating a photographic record of World War II. So, early in the autumn of 1941, I went to Washington and tried to interest the Air Force in reactivating my status as a reserve officer. When I arrived, the officer in charge took down my name and address politely, but when he came to the year of my birth, 1879, he put down his pen with an air of finality and told me he was sorry, but I was beyond the age limit for induction into active service.

After this discouraging refusal, I thought my only chance to be of service in photography would be as a civilian. So, as a start, I approached the camera clubs, as I had done early in World War I, with the idea of forming units to photograph the activities of the people and the country. Then David McAlpin, chairman of the Photography Committee and a Trustee of The Museum of Modern Art, approached me with the idea of doing an exhibition at the Museum. He assured me that I would have carte blanche. I conceived the idea of doing a contemporary portrait of America, with the title "The Arsenal of Democracy." I had begun collecting pictures for this exhibition when the attack on Pearl Harbor rocked the country. Then, more than ever, I felt my disappointment at not having been readmitted into the Air Force.

While I was in this state of deep discouragement, I received a telephone call from the Navy Department in Washington asking me if I would be interested in photographing for the Navy. I almost crawled through the telephone wire with eagerness. I replied that it so happened I had an appointment in Washington the next day.

I took a night train and, at an early hour, turned up at Naval Headquarters. I was heartily welcomed by Commander Arthur Doyle and was introduced to Captain A. W. Radford, who was then in command of training for naval aviators.

When I walked into Radford's office, I saw a look of surprise on his face. He had apparently not been informed that I was no longer a young man. Just then his telephone rang, and while he was talking I was saying to myself, "Boy, you've got to talk fast now." And the moment Captain Radford hung up, I started talking fast, telling him about my service in World War I and stressing my personal experiences under General Mitchell. This seemed to interest him very much, and I followed up quickly with a proposition. I told him I would like to head up a small unit of half a dozen photographers, commissioned by the Navy, to photograph the story of naval aviation during the war. This project interested Captain Radford. He took me to the Assistant Secretary of the Navy for Air to introduce me and to present the idea to him. Again I saw the shocked expression at my age, this time on the Secretary's face. Finally, he said to Captain Radford, "Well, if you really want him, I guess it's all right."

Captain Radford answered, as solemnly as a groom in a marriage ceremony, "I do."

I immediately started assembling a group of young photographers who were very divergent in their work and personalities. It took only a few weeks to select enough men to get the work of the unit organized, but, gradually, we added more photographers. Eventually the unit consisted of Wayne Miller, Charles Kerlee, Fenno Jacobs, Horace Bristol, Victor Jorgensen, Barrett Gallagher, and John Swope, all commissioned in the Navy, and Paul Dorsey, assigned to the unit from the Marine Corps. Navy Lieutenant Willard Mace served as executive assistant. In civilian life, the photographers had worked variously in journalism, documentary photography, illustration, advertising, and marine photography. Off duty, almost every one of them sooner or later came to me separately and said he understood why he had been chosen for the job, but he couldn't understand why some of the others had been.

I soon found that we were a rather irregular unit in the organizational setup of the Navy, and at first we met with opposition from the Navy's regular photographic service. Captain Radford, who soon became Admiral Radford, cleared this away and obtained for our photographers the freedom of movement and action necessary for good photography, but unprecedented in the Navy.

On our first job, we overcame a long-standing navy taboo. Before the war, it was considered undignified for an officer to carry a camera for making official photographs. All this work was assigned to noncommissioned personnel. But at the first naval air station our unit was assigned to photograph, each man turned up with several cameras slung around his shoulders and the usual kit bag of film and accessories. We were all officers, but no one challenged our right to carry a camera, then or at any time during our service.

I sent the men out on missions to various ships, usually aircraft carriers, since naval aviation was our job, and they all turned in exciting pictures. But curiously enough, although each man, in coming into the unit, had expressed enthusiasm for the freedom he would have in doing the kind of photography he wanted, he would invariably come to me before going on an assignment and ask, "Now, just what do you want me to do?"

My answer was always the same. "No one knows just what will happen in war. Photograph everything that happens, and you may find that you have made some historic photographs. But above all, concentrate on the men. The ships and planes will become obsolete, but the men will always be there."

Suddenly, just when naval operations were stepping up, I received a notice that I had reached the Navy's retirement age. Unwilling to retire, I reported this news to Secretary of the Navy James Forrestal, and the next day I was reinstated. But I was listed as disqualified for sea duty. I reported my distress to Admiral Radford, who was about to leave for Pearl Harbor to take charge of naval aviation operations there. He said he would send in a request for my services at Pearl Harbor. That would mean a sea operation was planned and I would go out on sea duty in connection with it. The order came. A junior officer, Victor Jorgensen, and I were to report to Pearl Harbor for temporary duty. When we arrived, we learned that a large navy task force was going to sea the very next morning.

Admiral Radford assigned us to the aircraft carrier *Lex-ington,* commanded by Captain, later Admiral, Felix Stump. Once at sea, I was informed by Captain Stump that we were going to the Gilbert and Marshall islands to cover the taking of Kwajalein Island by our Marines. I have told this story in full in *The Blue Ghost,* published by Harcourt, Brace and Company. It was illustrated with photographs that Jorgensen and I made on the trip.

Everything about an aircraft carrier is dramatic, but the most spectacular things are the take-offs and landings of the planes. In all the take-off pictures I had seen, the planes looked as though they were glued to the deck. They gave no impression of the terrific onrush as the planes started their run for the take-off. Nor did they suggest the noise, which is tremendous. Each thundering plane as it takes off emphasizes the contrast between the dynamic intensity of the moment at hand and the dreamlike memories of other places, other times, another life. It makes you aware that it's a cockeyed war in a cockeyed world, in which reality is piling up moments and images as fantastic and incongruous as those dished out by the Surrealists.

There was nothing I could do in the photographs to reproduce the sounds, but I was going to try to give a sense of the motion of the rushing plane. Instead of making a fast exposure to stop the motion and get a sharp picture of the plane taking off, I made a series of exposures around a tenth of a second. Plate 223 shows a Hellcat fighter plane taking off, its wheels just off the deck. Even the pilot is blurred, while the skipper on the bridge, in the upper left-hand corner, looks on like a benign Zeus.

The long voyage from Pearl Harbor to the Gilbert and Marshall islands was one of the trying things that military personnel always have to deal with: the long, long waiting for what's going to happen, with nothing to do about it. Things changed radically on the day before the Kwajalein Operation. Preparation for the strike brought feverish activity and an atmosphere of tenseness. In the ready room the pilots were being briefed, and on the deck the planes were being armed with bombs. To give an idea of the dramatic impact of the moment, I loaded my camera with infrared film that would darken the blue-gray of the carrier superstructure and the sky (plate 224).

After the successful Kwajalein Operation, we made a strike on another island. That night we were attacked by a fleet of land-based Japanese bombers and torpedo planes. The attack went on for almost seven hours, aided by bright moonlight and enemy flares which illuminated the entire task force. The *Lexington* was hit in the stern by a torpedo.

This locked our rudder on a sharp turn, and we traveled in circles, making a sitting-duck target; but somehow, we were not hit again. Unfortunately, no photographs were possible, because all lights were doused on the ships. The only way to photograph would have been with flash bulbs, and shooting off flash bulbs would probably have caused us to be dumped overboard by our crew. The *Lexington* was separated from the task force, but the task-force commander detailed a cruiser and a couple of destroyers to stay with us while we kept on making great circles. The engineer crew finally managed to straighten out the propeller, but we could not use the rudder. Steered only by the propeller, we made slow progress away from the scene of action.

I assumed that a ship struck by a torpedo would sink, so I tried to prepare a kit consisting of a dry camera and a supply of film placed inside an aerograph balloon. Jorgensen and I had planned this emergency procedure and had practiced inserting the camera in the balloon. With the two of us working, it was very easy. But working alone, all I could do was stretch open the balloon in one direction. Not having a third hand, I was not able to open it wide

enough to drop in the camera, which I held ready in my teeth.

I was on the bridge at the time. Captain Stump came along and asked me what I was doing. I told him I was trying to get my camera into the balloon so that I would have a dry camera when we abandoned ship. At this, the captain and the rest of the officers on the bridge burst into laughter. Unwittingly, I had served the purpose of breaking the tension. Captain Stump assured me we would remain afloat and there would be no call to abandon ship.

We limped back to Pearl Harbor, where temporary repairs were made, and then proceeded to the United States for the complete reconditioning of the ship.

I made another trip into the Pacific to Guam and Iwo Jima. I arrived in Iwo Jima the day after it was declared secure. That night, a number of fliers who had arrived the same day were killed by Japanese soldiers who came out from hiding places underground and dropped hand grenades into the tents of the sleeping men. Earlier that day, I had made the picture of a dead Japanese soldier, buried except for the fingertips either in a shell explosion or by a bulldozer (plate 225).

Shortly after this, Secretary Forrestal signed an order placing me in direct command of all navy combat photography.

223 *(below)* U.S.S. Carrier Lexington: Hellcat Goes Thundering off the Deck. 1943. U.S. Navy Photograph.
224 *(next page)* U.S.S. Carrier Lexington: Getting Set for the Big Strike on Kwajalein. 1943. U.S. Navy Photograph. Infra-red.

Although I was sixty-seven when I returned from active service in the Navy after World War II, I felt ready for another real job. During the war, I had organized two exhibitions, "Road to Victory" and "Power in the Pacific," for The Museum of Modern Art in New York City. My friend, Tom Maloney, the editor of *U.S. Camera Magazine* and *U.S. Camera Annual,* had published one book based on "Power in the Pacific" and another, *U.S. Navy War Photographs*. He had also given extensive magazine coverage to navy photography during the war. Tom spoke to Henry Allen Moe and Stephen Clark, trustees of The Museum of Modern Art, and to Alfred Barr, director of the Museum Collections, about my joining the staff of the Museum. The Board of Trustees created the position of director for the Department of Photography, and I was given the job.

I could not have dreamed up a more ideal proposition. This was the one museum that, on the initiative of Alfred Barr, from its inception had given photography more recognition than it had ever been accorded by any other institution in the world. As well as painting and sculpture and photography, the Museum also recognized the arts of architecture, design, and posters.

Actually, my first exhibition with The Museum of Modern Art had been held in 1936, and it was not an exhibition of photography but of my hybrid delphinium. This was the only time that living plant material had ever been shown at the Museum. By implication, flower breeding was recognized as one of the arts.

The delphinium exhibition brought a new audience to the Museum. On the opening day, all the prominent names in the world of horticulture turned up. The press gave it a good deal of space. The garden editor of the New York *Herald Tribune,* J.W. Johnston, came to the exhibition as a doubting Thomas, as did many of the professional horticultural fraternity. They were skeptical about the rather enthusiastic press releases sent out by the Museum. In his review, Mr. Johnston wrote: "In our brief existence, we had seen some delphinium that might be classed as highly creditable, and there must be a reasonable limit to what could be expected from the plant. Well, to put it conservatively, our standards have been raised at least fifty per cent by this. It is the most amazing exhibit of delphinium we have ever seen in this country by one man or by all

men and women put together. Here one man has proven again that with nature, almost anything is possible."

The exhibit was scheduled to run for about ten days, which meant we had to replace the delphinium twice, for they began to look tired after a few days in a hot spell. The Museum did not have air-conditioned galleries then. So on two occasions after the opening, we brought in several truckloads of blooms and refurbished the exhibition entirely.

The five-foot-long spikes of bloom were the big sensation to the general public. But to the experts, the pure blue delphinium spires, without any trace of lavender or violet, were the real sensation, because nothing like them had ever been seen. While most of the exhibition was devoted to the tall garden hybrids, I also included a small section of new interspecies crosses. One of these, a cross between the well-known garden variety, Belladonna, and a Chinese species, Tatsuenense, was the starting point of a new kind of delphinium in which very large flowers were produced on a graceful, bushlike plant rather than on tall, rigid spikes. I have since developed it further by the gradual introduction of the "blood" of other species and of the garden hybrids. I have given these new delphinium the name "Connecticut Yankees."

An unfortunate result of the Museum exhibition was the loss of my anonymity as a delphinium breeder, which I had cherished for twenty-six years.

My work with delphinium began in 1910, when I made my first crosses in connection with the great interest I had developed in heredity and genetics. Genetics was a very young science then. A practical plant breeder had little to go on, for the only scientific study in the field was the work of Abbé Gregor Mendel. His studies opened a new era of intensive research that has brought the science of genetics today to the verge of creating chemically some form of life.

The first photography exhibition I arranged after joining the staff of The Museum of Modern Art was drawn from what seemed to me the most promising and most vital area of photography, the field of documentary photojournalism. For this exhibition, I selected three young photographers, each presenting a theme. Wayne Miller contributed a series of pictures taken at the birth of his son. Leonard McCombe was represented with documentary records of war refugees in Berlin. And Homer Page showed an ironic commentary made during a convention of the American Legion. This was followed by an exhibition of five photographers working on a single theme, music. The first large exhibition, taking up a whole floor of the Museum, was "In and Out of Focus."

From the standpoint of representing the art of photography, probably the most comprehensive exhibition I organized for the Museum was that of photographs selected from the Permanent Collection. This exhibition not only presented a history of photography but also revealed the wealth of the Museum's collection of photographs. The collection was begun by Beaumont Newhall, the first curator of the Department of Photography. He set a standard for quality in his selection of prints that has been difficult to maintain and continues to be a goal to strive for. The Permanent Collection exhibition was historically important because it contained outstanding examples of all the best photographers from the earliest times to the present. Every school, every direction, every tendency, and all photographic processes were represented.

Another exhibition that I was particularly pleased to be able to introduce to the Museum's public was a showing by a large group of modern Japanese photographers. As a group, these photographers presented a coherence of esthetic and national traits in their work that no other nation has ever offered.

During my fifteen years as director of the Photography Department of the Museum, I organized forty-four exhibitions, in which were shown works by all the serious photographers from the beginning up to the outstanding contemporary workers in Europe, Japan, and the United States. The emphasis was almost always on the younger photographers.

A definite exception to this emphasis came in 1961, when, after some urging, the trustees of the Museum and the director, René d'Harnoncourt, persuaded me to have a retrospective exhibition of my own life's work in photography. In this case, "photography" was stretched to include the group of tempera paintings of the Oochens referred to in section 6. The exhibition was titled "Steichen the Photographer."

Photographers have always been concerned with the search for truth, according to their individual conceptions and abilities. This concern has also been true of the exhibitions at the Museum. In 1952, I began a series of group showings, actually groups of small one-man shows, presenting five or six photographers at a time under the title "Diogenes with a Camera." The purpose was to draw the attention of the public, as well as that of the photographers, to the rich diversity of interpretation present in the various modern photographers' searches for truth. Some of these exhibitions emphasized the diversity by contrasting the work of photographers whose pictures were naturalistic with that of photographers whose pictures ranged from a leaning toward abstraction to complete abstraction.

The genesis of the "theme" exhibitions produced at The Museum of Modern Art—"Road to Victory," "Power in the Pacific," "The Family of Man," and "The Bitter Years"—lay in the desire to have a series of photographs collectively communicate a significant human experience. This is something that an unrelated collection of even the finest photographs obviously cannot accomplish. Photography, including the cinema and television as well as the printed page, is a great and forceful medium of mass communication. To this medium the exhibition gallery adds still another dimension.

In the cinema and television, the image is revealed at a pace set by the director. In the exhibition gallery, the visitor sets his own pace. He can go forward and then retreat or hurry along according to his own impulse and mood as these are stimulated by the exhibition. In the creation of such an exhibition, resources are brought into play that are not available elsewhere. The contrast in scale of images, the shifting of focal points, the intriguing perspective of long- and short-range visibility with the images to come being glimpsed beyond the images at hand—all these permit the spectator an active participation that no other form of visual communication can give.

The creation of this kind of exhibition is more like the production of a play or novel, even a philosophical essay, than it is like planning an exhibition of pictures of individual works of art. Therefore, it must have an intrinsic aim that gives it an element of the universal and an over-all unity. It should also have an existence of its own, as does any other work of art. An exhibition of this nature is not necessarily limited to photography, but the technical and practical aspects of photography make it eminently suitable. The ease with which any given image can be made small or large, the flexibility of placement and juxtaposition, the great range of material available in photographs—all these factors make photography the obvious medium for such projects. No amount of technical bravura, however, can make up for the lack of a fundamental idea from which the exhibition must grow. There must first be a desire to convey a feeling or a thought about a moment or a condition, to build upon the elements furnished by nature and the experiences amassed in the art of living, and to orchestrate these into a unified force.

"The Family of Man" was the most important undertaking of my career. In a way, it had its genesis in the several war exhibitions I had organized. I had banked particularly on the last of these, the Korean War exhibition, to make a thought-provoking impression on the world, for this war had undergone a more realistic photographic interpretation than any other. The exhibition was dominated by the work of David Douglas Duncan, whose book *This Is War* is the most forceful indictment of the subject ever put forth by photography. I stated in my premise for the exhibition that "that war really dumped a place and a time called Korea into our very laps." People flocked in great numbers to see it. They found some pictures revolting, some deeply moving. There even were tears shed, but that was as far as it went. They left the exhibition and promptly forgot it.

Although I had presented war in all its grimness in three exhibitions, I had failed to accomplish my mission. I had not incited people into taking open and united action against war itself. This failure made me take stock of my fundamental idea. What was wrong? I came to the conclusion that I had been working from a negative approach, that what was needed was a positive statement on what a wonderful thing life was, how marvelous people were, and, above all, how alike people were in all parts of the world.

My first concept was in the direction of human rights, but I soon realized that this also had negative implications. And, at that time, the subject of human rights was becoming an international political football. The real need was for an expression of the oneness of the world we lived in. One day, while thumbing through Carl Sandburg's Lincoln biography, I ran across a speech in which Lincoln used the term "family of man." Here was the all-embracing theme for the exhibition.

The Museum's trustees accepted a synopsis of the project and offered to guarantee the considerable expenses of the production.

Before undertaking the project, I wanted to make certain it could be realized. I was confident that American photographers could supply a good coverage of America and many other parts of the world, but I wanted to make certain that European photographers could be counted on. In 1952, I made a survey trip to Europe and visited twenty-nine cities in eleven countries. As a result, I was convinced that the exhibition was possible.

It was the most challenging project the world's photographers had ever met. The Museum engaged Wayne Miller as my assistant. We circulated our requests for photographs to magazines, clubs, and societies, as well as to individual photographers all over the world. Later, I was able to use the text of this request almost intact in the prologue I wrote for the exhibition and the book. In addition to the photographs that arrived in response to our invitation, Wayne Miller personally went through more than two million photographs in various collections in the country. We amassed a preliminary collection of about ten thousand prints, and from these we selected the material to make up the exhibition.

Eliminating half of these pictures was comparatively easy, but further reductions became increasingly difficult. The final reduction from one thousand to five hundred, which was the number considered the limit for the exhibition, became a real struggle and was often heartbreaking. It involved the necessary elimination of many fine photographs.

The next step was to make up the major themes from all the material selected and to develop a sequence. For this work, the Museum rented a loft for us in a building on Fifty-Second Street. Since the building was about to be demolished, the landlord took down some partitions, and we had one very large room and one tiny back room, which was furnished with an army cot. Here I could take an occasional rest or spend the night. It was not always the quiet night one could hope for, since, on the ground floor, there was a striptease joint with a wangy orchestra grinding out the same tunes night after night until three o'clock in the morning.

We had a fine staff of assistants who went through the files again and again in search of suitable material for weak sections. This staff consisted of Miss Kathleen Haven, Mrs. Wayne Miller, Miss Doris O'Donnell, and Mrs. Donald Honeyman. Of the several architects suggested by the Museum's staff to design the installation, I had concluded from the beginning that Paul Rudolph was the right man. My confidence was based on his imagination and understanding, and, above all, his superb sense of design.

The final selection consisted of five hundred and three photographs representing sixty-eight countries. Monroe Wheeler, the Museum's director of Exhibitions and Publications, announced that we should have a book about the exhibition. I favored having two editions of the book. One would be a handsome edition containing the best possible reproductions and printing; it would serve as a permanent record. The other would be a paperback edition that would sell for not more than one dollar. As we selected the pictures, we had pinned them up in sequence on panels running around the big room of the loft. A number of publishers were brought in to see this material, and our discouragement was almost complete when they all turned it down.

One day I met my friend Jerry Mason and told him of our disappointment. He asked if he could come to see the material. I invited him in, and after spending several hours carefully studying the photographs, Mason said he would like to do the book. I sent him over to Wheeler at the Museum. Wheeler was impressed with Mason's enthusiasm and his evident faith in the material as a book. Jerry Mason was told to go ahead and draw up a proposition. When I met Mason a few days later, he said he was ready to do the book. He was particularly interested in the dollar edition, which he said he would produce himself through his outfit, the Maco Press. He said he was going to print a first edition of 135,000 copies. I promptly protested. "Jerry," I said, "you're crazy. We can't let you do that. You'll lose your shirt." So I automatically became a confederate of the doubting publishers who had turned down the book!

Mason went ahead, with the blessings of the Museum, and the first thing he did was to sell the production of the de luxe edition to Simon and Schuster, who had originally turned the project down firmly. Donnelley and Company, in Chicago, undertook the job of reproducing and printing the pictures on high-speed rotary presses. I believe the work they did stands today without a peer among achieve-

ments by this process. Donnelley also made reproductions for the de luxe book, which was printed on a heavier paper and made by sheet-fed gravure. The de luxe edition was sold out within a few months of publication. The paper-covered version also sold out, of course, and the presses of Donnelley have been kept busy turning out editions ever since. Today, over two million copies of *The Family of Man* have been sold in the original size, plus half a million copies of a still smaller Pocket Books edition, printed by another printer and engraver.

The "Family of Man" exhibition was opened to the public in January 1955. It broke all the Museum's records for attendance at its exhibitions of contemporary arts. The Museum circulated the original edition of the show and a smaller-scale version throughout the United States. The United States Information Agency took it over for showing abroad and eventually circulated six separate editions. The Compo Photocolor Company produced the fine prints and murals for the original exhibition at the Museum, and also made up and refurbished the six traveling editions. To date, the exhibition has been seen by more than nine million people in sixty-nine countries, and it is still being shown.

Japan independently made up four editions of the exhibition in different sizes for showing throughout the country. The smallest size was scaled for showing in villages. More than a million people saw "The Family of Man" in Japan. Another million saw it in India, in one of the U.S.I.A. editions. In every country and every city where the exhibition was shown, it was seen by record audiences and received unprecedented space in the press. From each country, the United States Information Service sent back reports saying this was the best thing the United States had ever sent out. The press reviews in several countries said it was particularly gratifying that this exhibition had originated in the United States.

"The Family of Man" appealed to all kinds of audiences, the illiterate as well as the intelligentsia, who, in some areas, gave it unqualified endorsement. In Paris, a city that is ordinarily glutted with exhibitions, "The Family of Man" had its greatest press reception. From the socialist *L'Humanité* to the conservative *Le Figaro* and *Le Temps,* the expressions of enthusiasm were the same. Paris papers had double-page spreads of pictures followed by columns of text.

A notable experience was reported from Guatemala. On the final day of the exhibition, a Sunday, several thousand Indians from the hills of Guatemala came on foot or muleback to see it. An American visitor said it was like a religious experience to see these barefoot country people who could not read or write walk silently through the exhibition gravely studying each picture with rapt attention.

No one had even suspected anything like the reception accorded to "The Family of Man" across the world. I have personally seen the exhibition in four nations and seven cities. I have watched the reaction of the various peoples and found that, regardless of the place, the response was always the same. I finally came to the conclusion that the deep interest in this show was based on a kind of audience participation. The people in the audience looked at the pictures, and the people in the pictures looked back at them. They recognized each other. A Japanese poet has said that, when you look into a mirror, you do not see your reflection, your reflection, sees you.

As far as I was concerned, the high spot of the project was the 1959 showing in Moscow. Carl Sandburg and I were sent over by the State Department to attend the opening of the big American Exhibition in Gorki Park. "The Family of Man" was part of it. Carl and I attended the official opening and sat on the platform with Premier Khrushchev, Vice-President Nixon, the American ambassador, and other dignitaries. We were faced with a battery of cameras—television, movie, and still—and I had with me a small Minox Camera, which, every now and then, I pointed at the photographers.

Russian audiences were led through the "Family of Man" exhibition by a young American guide named Martin Horwitz. In fluent Russian, he gave a general discourse on the exhibition and answered questions about the individual pictures. He played a big role in the Russian people's feeling about the exhibition.

I made a number of snapshots while the exhibition was in Russia. I stood in one spot for about twenty minutes and photographed the people as they looked at the section devoted to parents and babies (plates 234–237). I decided that, if I were to say the snapshots had been made in Wisconsin or Iowa or New England, the statement would be accepted without question.

The Moscow press ignored "The Family of Man" until the day before the whole American Exhibition closed. Then, *Pravda* published an article almost a full page long about "The Family of Man," and except for some satire, the report was rather favorable. The satire was expressed in complaints that the exhibition did not reveal certain "necessary" statistics. For instance, we should have given the figures on how many more babies died in Timbuctoo than in New York or Chicago.

I was asked if I wanted to meet any of the Russian photographers, and I said I was particularly anxious to do so, but I wanted to meet professional photographers, the journalists, not the so-called art photographers. A meeting of about twenty or twenty-five men was arranged. One of the first questions they asked was why there were so few Russian pictures in "The Family of Man." I explained that the circular requesting contributions from the U.S.S.R. had been sent to the Ministry of Culture in Moscow, and the Ministry had sent back two big batches of photographs, all arty pictures of the subway, the bridges, and some of the buildings in Leningrad, but no pictures of the one subject we had asked for, the Russian people. I explained that I didn't think the Russian journalist photographers had been represented in the pictures we received. The few pictures of Russian situations that were used in "The Family of Man" had been found by Wayne Miller in the files of Sovfoto, a Russian organization in New York.

Then, two of the Russians who had pictures in "The Family of Man" identified themselves at the meeting. I told them I had sent the first batches of pictures back to Moscow, explaining that there must be some misunderstanding and enclosing another circular with the important parts underscored. Very soon, another big box of photographs had arrived. While they were not duplicates, they were exactly like the first lot that had been sent. Again, there were no pictures of the Russian people.

In another question, I was told that apparently I didn't take much interest in abstract photography, because there was none of it in "The Family of Man." I replied that "The Family of Man" was an exhibition in which abstract photography did not have a place. But we did exhibit abstract photographs at our Museum. Then I told them how I felt about abstract photography. I said that, when young photographers came to the Museum to show me their abstract photographs, I told them they must realize that they might be working along a blind alley. However, as long as they wanted to work in abstraction, I would fight for their right to do so and would encourage them in their work. This brought a murmur of approval.

I also met some of the young painters who delved into the realm of the abstract. No one seemed to interfere with what they were doing, but these painters were working in a vacuum, because they had no way of showing their work and no way of knowing what was going on in the rest of the world.

We also met various members of the Union of Writers of the U.S.S.R. Some were very stuffy, but there were a few whom it was a real pleasure to meet. One was a woman, Frieda Lurie, a translator of American literature into Russian. She spoke English perfectly, and she was a most gracious and charming person. But the most important figure I met was the poet Yevgeny Yevtushenko.

I spent several afternoons and evenings with Yevtushenko. Usually, when one talked to any of the literary intelligentsia and the conversation started to be free and open, it would end with a change of subject as abrupt as a curtain being pulled down. With Yevtushenko we spoke very freely. However, if there was any talk that compared the artists in America with those in Russia, he was vigorous in his defense of the Soviet artists.

Yevtushenko was as devoted a Soviet citizen as any I met, but he was open-minded toward opposite points of view. He was critical of the abstract paintings in the American Exhibition. To him they were abstruse and incomprehensible. When I said that the artist was frequently ahead of his time, Yevtushenko said, "No, the artist should be like a locomotive. He pulls the people in the train along with him."

Later, when we were visiting the studio of a friend of his, a portrait painter, the artist showed us a portrait of a woman who, Yevtushenko said, was one of the great poets of Russia. During her lifetime she had been mocked and derided, but now she was recognized as a great artist. I said this was one time when the locomotive had run away from the train. Yevtushenko laughed heartily.

During the two weeks that Carl Sandburg and I were in Russia, I probably met and talked to more Russian people at "The Family of Man" exhibition than I could have met and talked to in two years under ordinary conditions. These contacts left me with the impression that the Russian people were more like Americans than the people of any other country I have visited. I was also left with the impression, however, that everyone I met in Moscow was convinced that the Soviet system of government was superior to any other in the world.

When we landed in Stockholm on our way home from Moscow, I suddenly became conscious that, for the first time in two weeks, I was breathing freely again. Freedom is something that is in the air of a country.

226–230 (opposite) "The Family of Man." Editing the Exhibition. New York. 1954.
Photographs by Wayne Miller and Homer Page.

231–233 *(opposite and above)* "The Family of Man" at The Museum of Modern Art. New York. 1955.
Installation designed by the architect Paul Rudolf.
Photographs by Ezra Stoller.

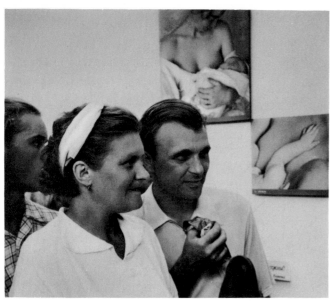

234–237 "The Family of Man" in Moscow. 1959.
Snapshots by Edward Steichen.

When I took over the job as director of photography at The Museum of Modern Art, I decided I could not do a satisfactorily objective job if I were an active photographer myself. So I laid aside my own photographic work. One day when I was looking over a young photographer's work and discussing it with him, I discovered how effective my decision had been. At one point he asked me if I had ever made any photographs myself!

During the last five or six years of my work at the Museum, the itch to photograph again became so strong that I decided I would have to do something about it. I assigned myself a disciplined third apprenticeship. I limited myself to photographing what could be seen from the windows of our home in Redding, Connecticut.

One spring, from the window of my bedroom I noticed a little shad-blow tree in full bloom. I remembered I had planted the tree twenty or twenty-five years before, when it was no more than a foot high, but this was the first time I had observed it in bloom. From then on, I concentrated on the little shad-blow tree. For the next three or four years, I photographed it on 35-mm color film in every season and at all hours of the day.

After accumulating several hundred pictures of the little shad-blow, I tried to weave them into a consecutive series, thinking of it as a concerto, with the little tree the solo instrument and the neighboring trees and pond the members of the orchestra. In projecting the pictures as slides, however, I found that the interruption between each slide made the flow of any sustained mood impossible. One evening when I was showing the series to Pare Lorentz and his wife, Elizabeth Meyer Lorentz, they had the same reaction. They wondered about each picture separately as it was shown. I mentioned that this was my usual experience and a great disappointment to me. So Lorentz, like the great documentary film-man he is, immediately suggested that I transfer these pictures onto movie film and let one dissolve into the other.

This struck me as a good idea. But then I thought, why turn these still pictures into a film? Why not start the series over again as a motion picture and take advantage of the wind and the rain and the movements of the water? On movie film, I could also have the advantage of sound by recording the noises of wind and of rain splashing on the

water and the sounds of birds, frogs, and insects. So I began again with an Ariflex movie camera and worked for about two years. Now I feel that it will take at least another two years to complete this photographic concerto.

The pictures reproduced in plates 238 through 241 and 243 through 248 are from the still Kodachrome shots.

One day, while I was making some black-and-white photographs of sunlight sparkling on the water of the pond in front of the shad-blow tree, I looked around and saw Joanna watching me from the living-room window. The sparkling sunlight I had been photographing was reflected in the window, so I swung around with my camera and made the picture in plate 249.

In July 1962, after fifteen years as director of the Department of Photography at The Museum of Modern Art, I retired and left the future operation of the department to the direction of John Szarkowski and the curatorship of Grace M. Mayer. There remained, however, an exhibition I long had wanted to do. It was "The Bitter Years," a review of some of the photographs made for the United States Government by the Farm Security Administration photographers under the direction of Roy Stryker. These photographs covered the plight of the American farmer from 1935 to 1941. In 1962 the time seemed ripe for a reminder of those "bitter years" and for bringing them into the consciousness of a new generation that had problems of its own but was largely unaware of the endurance and fortitude that had made the emergence from the Great Depression one of America's victorious hours.

We were living now with the continuing Cold War between East and West and with the almost daily threat of race suicide through the nuclear bomb. We had recently seen near-panic over a stock market that dropped swiftly from a dizzy altitude and made too many citizens feel discouraged and sorry for themselves. The image of stamina presented by our people during the "bitter years" of another critical period might perform a revitalizing function.

Another reason for producing "The Bitter Years" was the peerless quality of this particular photographic document. It seemed that to show this unique project now might awaken interest in the establishment of a permanent photographic organization to document continually all phases and activities of the United States and its people.

The most precious factor in the creative life of an artist in any medium is freedom. Totalitarian, political, or national ideologies that seek to direct or channel the arts are pernicious; they can strangle the work of individual artists and cripple their own culture. They are not, however, the only things that hamper an artist's freedom. It can also be curtailed by commercial conditions or by the theories of aesthetics ordained by various groups, cults, cliques, or "isms." But it seems to me that the most damaging restrictions on an artist's liberty are self-imposed. So often, what may have begun as fresh thinking and discovery is turned into a routine and reduced to mere habit. Habits in thinking or technique are always stultifying in the long run. They are also contagious, and when a certain set of habits becomes general, a whole art period can condemn itself to the loss of freedom. It is probably this stultifying process, more than anything else, that transforms the avant-garde of one generation into academicians in the eyes of the next.

During its relatively brief existence, the art of photography has been miraculously successful in resisting all attempts at being "frozen" into a philosophy or ideology or system of aesthetics. The only movement that ever did hold sway for any length of time went by the name "pictorial photography"—whatever that may have meant. It would appear that, at one time, American photographers deplored their comparative backwardness in this so-called pictorial photography. Sometime during the 1890s, when Stieglitz was editor of the magazine *American Amateur Photographer,* he used a printed rejection slip which he sent out to photographers who submitted work for publication. The rejection slip read, "Technically excellent. Pictorially rotten." Although the term "pictorial" never had a definite meaning in its time, it seemed to be concerned with the idea of making attractive pictures rather than documentary records. This idea appealed to the camera clubs, and even now some of the clubs and the photographic societies advocate it. But to the serious photographer of today, the term "pictorial" is anathema.

Some photographic movements have had a following in America, but none has ever held sway for any length of time. The Photo-Secession, documentary photography, photo-journalism, f/64, all made valuable individual contributions, but they all had to give way to the self-assertive individual photographer. Of course, individual photographers do bind themselves to certain limiting systems of aesthetics, as well as to habits, from time to time, but when they are good photographers, this debilitating condition does not last long.

An individual photographer sometimes gives up his basic freedom out of an excess of admiration for the work of another photographer or other artists. But another, even more destructive loss of freedom comes from an overflow of egoism, when the ego spills over and expresses itself as conceit. Of course, excessive humility can also be a weakness impinging on freedom, but in every great artist humility is always an important part of his attitude toward nature and toward his medium. This kind of humility opens doors and vistas, whereas conceit shuts them tight.

In the vigorous state of present-day photography, we have such a multitude of varying concepts that there is little danger of any of them taking over the banner of righteousness and imposing its aesthetic upon the others. In the past few years there has been a larger number of free-spirited, independently thinking young photographers —seekers, probers, and explorers of new horizons—than we have heretofore encountered. They give ample assurance that the future of photography is richer in prospect and potential than ever before. They present a welcome lack of self-satisfaction, emulation, or complacency.

Having carried out the promise I made to Alfred Stieglitz when I was twenty-one, that I would always stick to photography, it is with particular pleasure that, today at eighty-four, I warmly salute—with a "Good luck, and keep at it!"—the present young generation of photographers.

238-241 The Shad-Blow Tree. Umpawaug, Connecticut. 1955. From 35 mm. Kodachrome.

242 Dana Miller in the Pond. Umpawaug, Connecticut. 1954.

242 Dana Miller in the Pond. Umpawaug, Connecticut. 1954.

243-248 *(above and next two pages)* The Shad-Blow Tree.
Umpawaug, Connecticut. From 35 mm. Kodachrome.

249 Joanna (Mrs. Edward Steichen). Umpawaug, Connecticut. 1959.

graphs in exhibition at National Arts Club, N. Y., March 12 to April 2: One-man show of photographs in monochrome and color at The Photo-Secession. April: Three Lumière Autochromes by Steichen are reproduced in *Camera Work* (No. 22). April 15–22: One-man show of paintings and photographs at Pratt Institute. *Everybody's Magazine* commissions him to photograph Theodore Roosevelt and William Howard Taft, paying the unprecedented sum of $500 each for reproduction rights. June 15: Marriage of Lillian Steichen and Carl Sandburg. Late September: Photographs Rodin's *Balzac*.

1909 February 2–20: Included in "International Photography" exhibition at National Arts Club. April 21–May 7: Steichen's *Balzac-Moonlight* Series shown at The Little Gallery of The Photo-Secession (moved across the hall from the original quarters). Three photographs later reproduced in Rodin Number of *Camera Work* (34–35, April–July, 1911). May–October; 30 Steichen prints in "The 'International Group' at The Dresden Exhibition."

1910 January 21–February 5: His color photographs shown at The Photo-Secession Gallery concurrently with his exhibition of 31 paintings and 28 photographs at the Montross Gallery, New York (January 17–29). March 21–April 15: Included in group show "The Younger American Painters" at The Photo-Secession Gallery. Studies genetics, and begins hybridizing delphinium in his gardens at Voulangis, France. November 4 to December 1: 31 prints by Steichen included in the "International Exhibition of Pictorial Photography" at the Albright Art Gallery, Buffalo—the last important show sponsored by The Photo-Secession. December 11–31: Exhibition of paintings by Eduard Steichen at the Worcester (Mass.) Art Museum.

1911 Urged by Lucien Vogel to make fashion a fine art through photography; 13 Steichen photographs of Paul Poiret creations unprecedentedly used to illustrate "L'Art de la Robe," by Paul Cornu, in April issue of *Art et Décoration* (Paris). Begins painting large mural decorations for home of Mr. and Mrs. Eugene Meyer, Jr. Concentrates on painting for several years.

1913 Tentatively begins series of experimental photographs of plant forms, flowers, and insects. Double Number of *Camera Work* (42–43, April–July, 1913) is devoted to Steichen, to whom Stieglitz, signing himself "291," writes on November 26: "This is the first copy of the 'Steichen Number.' It is just out. It happens to be the night before Thanksgiving. Nothing I have ever done has given me quite so much satisfaction as finally sending this Number out into the world...."

1914 Returns with family to New York upon outbreak of World War I. Sends sharply critical reply to Stieglitz's circularized inquiry, "What is '291'?", for inclusion in *Camera Work* (Number 47, July, 1914; published January, 1915).

1915 January 25–February 6: Exhibition entitled "Paintings by Eduard J. Steichen" at M. Knoedler & Co., New York, includes 21 canvases and 7 "Mural Decorations Painted for Mr. and Mrs. Eugene Meyer, Jr. Motive: – In Exaltation of Flowers." March: Contributes to "291"—A New Publication (Editorial Board: Alfred Stieglitz, Marius de Zayas, and Agnes Meyer), with drawing "What Is Rotten In The State Of Denmark?" reproduced on back page of No. 1, and "Le Coq Gaulois" in the May issue (No. 3).

1917– Volunteers and is commissioned First Lieutenant in U.S. Army,
1919 July, 1917. Arrives in France with American Expeditionary Force on day after Rodin's death, November 17, 1917. Made Chevalier of Legion of Honor; receives Medaille d'Honneur des Affaires Etrangères; also Distinguished Service Citation from General Pershing. Remains in Army one year following Armistice to establish Aviation Photography on a permanent basis. Retired with rank of Lt. Colonel October 31, 1919. Wartime experience in development of aerial photography revitalizes and broadens his concept of photography as an art.

1919– At Voulangis begins study of ratios of plant growth as a basis
1922 for discipline. Begins photographing objects to convey abstract meanings, and makes experimental abstract paintings on Chinese symbol of Yen and Yan. Decides to renounce painting and concentrate on photography; burns all canvases remaining in Voulangis studio.

1921 Goes to Athens with Isadora Duncan and her pupils; photographs them on the Acropolis.

1923 March 28: Begins work for Condé Nast Publications as Chief Photographer, photographs appearing regularly in *Vogue* and *Vanity Fair* (1923–38). Commences advertising photography for J. Walter Thompson Co. Marries Dana Desboro Glover. Takes studio in Beaux Arts Building, 80 West 40th Street, New York.

1924 Experiments with Howard M. Edmunds' machine to make sculpture from photographs. Gives up home at Voulangis.

1926– Successfully brings suit (financed by Mrs. Harry Payne Whit-
1928 ney) against the U.S. Government, to prove that Brancusi's *Bird in Space* (which he had purchased from the sculptor) is a work of art. Court orders return of duty Steichen had paid.

1928 Establishes Umpawaug Plant Breeding Farm at West Redding, Connecticut, and again starts breeding delphinium.

1929 *Steichen The Photographer* by Carl Sandburg published by Harcourt, Brace and Co., New York.

1930 Collaborates with daughter, Mary Steichen Martin (later Dr. Calderone) to produce *The First Picture Book: Everyday Things For Babies* (Harcourt, Brace and Co., New York).

1931 *The Second Picture Book* appears. Made Honorary Fellow of The Royal Photographic Society of Great Britain.

1932 Exhibits photomurals of the George Washington Bridge in "Murals by American Painters and Photographers" directed by Julien Levy—the first showing of photography and of Steichen's work at The Museum of Modern Art. May 22, Edward Alden Jewell, of the *Times* Art Department, rates Steichen's contribution as "... at once architectural in composition and thanks to a daring play of values, grandiose, tremendous in its decorative and emotional appeal." Designs photomurals for Center Theatre, Radio City, New York.

1933 Designs photomurals for the New York State Building at the Chicago World's Fair ("Century of Progress"). Death of mother.

1934 Moves studio to 139 East 69th Street.

1935 Selects photographs for *U.S. Camera Annuals,* which he continues to do until 1947. Designs four pieces of glass executed by Steuben (c. 1935).

1936 Displays his hybrid delphinium at The Museum of Modern Art.

1937 Receives Silver Medal Award (Annual Advertising Awards) "In Recognition Of His Distinguished Service To Advertising."

1938 January 1: Closes studio at 139 East 69th Street. During vacation in Mexico, starts using 35-mm. Contax, photographing in color. June 1–30: One-man retrospective exhibition of 150 prints at Baltimore Museum of Art.

1940 Receives the Art Directors Club Medal.

Biographical Outline

Compiled by Grace M. Mayer, Curator, The Department of Photography, The Museum of Modern Art. Reprinted, condensed, with revisions and additions, from *Steichen the Photographer,* New York: The Museum of Modern Art, 1961. Distributed by Doubleday & Company, Inc.

1879 March 27: Eduard Jean Steichen born in Luxembourg, only son of Marie Kemp and Jean-Pierre Steichen.

1881 Family settles in Hancock, Michigan, where father works in copper mines and mother trims hats.

1883 Sister Lillian (the future Mrs. Carl Sandburg) born.

1888 Sent to Pio Nono College near Milwaukee, where teacher's praise of his drawings gives mother the hope he will become an artist.

1889 Family moves to Milwaukee.

1893 Earnings help to defray cost of trip to World's Columbian Exposition in Chicago, where he becomes absorbed in the production and use of electricity.

1894– Formal education ends at 15. Begins 4-year apprenticeship in
1898 a Milwaukee lithographing company. In 1897 wins prize for design of envelope for National Educational Association Convention in Milwaukee. Organizes and becomes first President of Milwaukee Art Students' League.

1899 Initial recognition as photographer comes at first public showing in the Second Philadelphia Salon (October 21–November 19).

1900 His entries in the Chicago Salon (April 3–18) evoke letter of encouragement from Clarence H. White, who also writes to Alfred Stieglitz about him. After 21st birthday, passes through New York en route abroad. Goes to the Camera Club of New York to see Stieglitz, who buys three of his prints. In Paris goes to l'Exposition Universelle, where Rodin's work makes profound impression. Takes Latin Quarter studio. September 21–November 3: Earliest representation in the London Photographic Salon. Goes to London for his first large showing (21 prints) in exhibition of "The New School of American Photography" organized by F. Holland Day and held by The Royal Photographic Society (October 10–November 8). Represented in Third Philadelphia Salon (October 22–November 18).

1901 February 22–March 10: "The New School of American Photography" exhibition (with Steichen's share augmented to 35 prints) travels to Paris. Steichen's painting, "Portrait of F. Holland Day," included in Paris "Salon de 1901." Autumn: Taken to meet Rodin at his Meudon home. Is elected a member of the "Linked Ring," the more advanced photographic society of London.

1902 James Huneker (in *The Sun,* March 12, 1902) declares Steichen's 14 prints in the exhibition of "American Pictorial Photography. Arranged by The 'Photo-Secession'" at the National Arts Club in New York (March 5–22), "the star exhibit in this collection" and of his portraits writes "… it is probably not an exaggeration to say that they represent the highest point to which photographic portraiture has yet been brought." Becomes one of the founders of The Photo-Secession, and designs the cover of *Camera Work,* its famed quarterly voice from 1903–17. Sunday, March 30: *The New York Herald* carries the following: "PHOTOGRAPHS IN THE SALON Innovation To Be Introduced for First Time in Paris Art Exhibition." June 3–24: Steichen's first

one-man show of paintings and photographs held at La Maison des Artistes, Paris. Midsummer: Returns to New York impoverished and takes the 291 Fifth Avenue studio which was to become in 1905 "The Little Galleries of the Photo-Secession," subsequently known as "291." Here he initiated the idea of showing works of art in all media, to begin with an exhibition of Rodin's drawings. Steichen's photograph, "The Black Vase," is purchased by the Belgian Government.

1903 January 31: The President's Cup of the Camera Club of New York presented to "Newcomer" (Eduard J. Steichen) for his photograph of Bartholomé. April: The Steichen Number of *Camera Work,* for which Maeterlinck writes an appreciation, appears. Wins top prize in Eastman Kodak Competition, Special Commendation in the Wiesbaden (Germany) Awards and First Prize in Portrait Class in the Bausch & Lomb Quarter-century Competition. October 3: Marries Clara E. Smith (two daughters: Dr. Mary Calderone and Kate Rodina Steichen). Photographs J.P. Morgan and Eleonora Duse in one morning.

1904 January: Exhibits at the Corcoran Gallery of Art, Washington, D.C., and (February) at the Carnegie Institute, Pittsburgh, in the Photo-Secession Exhibition. Photograph "Rodin—Le Penseur" receives prize for "best picture" in International Exhibition at The Hague. Takes his first color photographs (1904–5) with three-color separations with a repeating-back camera.

1905 February 25–March 10: The showing of 29 of his paintings at the Galleries of Eugene Glaenzer and Co., New York, proves outstanding success. Collaborates with Alfred Stieglitz in organizing and establishing The Photo-Secession Galleries in his former studio, 291 Fifth Avenue. Envisions exhibition there of works in all media as well as photography. Designs galleries and installations. November 24–January 5 (1906): His photographs included in opening exhibition. Awarded two First Prizes in Eastman Kodak Competition and First Prize in The Goerz Competition.

1906 March 16–31: Exhibition of Photographs by Eduard Steichen (including experiments in three-color photography) at The Photo-Secession. April: The Steichen Number and Special Steichen Supplement to *Camera Work* appear. Edition de Luxe, known as "The Steichen Book," issued. April 30–May 27: Participates in "An Exhibition of Photographs arranged by the Photo-Secession" at Pennsylvania Academy of the Fine Arts, Philadelphia. Early May: Returns to France. Selects Rodin drawings for exhibition at The Photo-Secession.

1907 Steichen invests in Lumière Autochrome Plates, and within a week achieves startling results. His color transparencies included in the Members' Show at The Photo-Secession Galleries. Returns to New York with Rodin drawings.

1908 January 2: Initiates showings of modern art in America with exhibition of "Drawings by Auguste Rodin" at The Photo-Secession Galleries, directed by Alfred Stieglitz. Other European artists and American painters resident in Paris (where Steichen had established "The New Society of Younger American Painters") were subsequently introduced in the same galleries in series of exhibitions initiated by Steichen: Matisse, 1908; Alfred Maurer and John Marin, 1909; Cézanne, 1910; E. Gordon Craig, 1910; Max Weber, 1911; Picasso, 1911; Arthur B. Carles, 1912; and Constantin Brancusi, 1914 (all dates refer to first showings). January: Steichen paintings and photo-

1941 Invited by Captain (now Admiral) Arthur W. Radford to form small unit of photographers to photograph Naval Aviation.

1942 Commissioned Lt. Commander, USNR. Creates a new photo exhibition concept, "Road to Victory," with text by Carl Sandburg and installation design by Herbert Bayer. Edward Alden Jewell, Art Critic of *The New York Times,* on May 21 calls it "breathtaking and poignantly memorable... a portrait of a nation, heroic in stature." In a Sunday reprise (May 24) Jewell writes: "a moving and gigantic camera chronicle of America today.... For one thing, photography, as here demonstrated, has... turned a corner.... And if photo murals of such power and splendor as these have been produced in the past, I have not seen them." May 17: Receives Honorary Master of arts Degree from Wesleyan University.

1943 November 9–December 23: Aboard the Carrier U.S.S. *Lexington* during the Gilbert and Marshall Islands Operation.

1944 Supervises U.S. Navy film, *The Fighting Lady.*

1945 Named Director of U.S. Navy Photographic Institute and placed in command of all Navy Combat Photography by James Forrestal, Secretary of the Navy. Awarded Distinguished Service Medal. Receives Honorary Fellowship, P.S.A. Creates exhibition "Power in the Pacific" (designed by Lt. G. E. Kidder-Smith, USNR) for The Museum of Modern Art (January 23–March 20); show recorded in book form (U.S. Camera Publishing Corp., New York). April: Receives The Art Directors Club Medal for his work on *The Fighting Lady.*

1946 January 30: Released from active duty in the Navy, with rank of Captain. Compiles book, *U.S. Navy War Photographs: Pearl Harbor to Tokyo Harbor* (U.S. Camera, New York).

1947 July: Becomes Director of Department of Photography of The Museum of Modern Art. Relinquishes own photography to obtain more objectivity in judging the work of others. *The Blue Ghost,* a word-and-picture account of his U.S.S. *Lexington* experience, published by Harcourt, Brace and Co. Starts his Museum exhibition program, which Jacob Deschin later praised in *Say It With Your Camera* (McGraw-Hill Book Co., Inc., 1950). Exhibitions: "Three Young Photographers; Leonard McCombe, Wayne Miller, Homer Page"; "Music and Musicians."

1948 Exhibitions: "In and Out of Focus"; "50 Photographs by 50 Photographers"; "Photo-Secession Group"; "Four Photographers: Lisette Model, Bill Brandt, Ted Croner, and Harry Callahan."

1949 Receives U.S. Camera Achievement Award for the "most outstanding contribution to photography by an individual." Exhibitions: "The Exact Instant"; "Roots of Photography: Hill-Adamson, Cameron"; "Realism in Photography: Ralph Steiner, Wayne Miller, Tosh Matsumoto, and Frederick Sommer"; "Six Women Photographers: Margaret Bourke-White, Helen Levitt, Dorothea Lange, Tana Hoban, and Hazel and Frieda Larsen"; "Roots of French Photography."

1950 May: Retrospective exhibition at American Institute of Architects Headquarters, Washington, D.C. May 10: "The American Institute of Architects welcomes a fresh skill in the use of scientific lens and film—welcomes a Master of Photography, and awards its Fine Arts Medal to Edward Steichen, thus acclaiming another art to grace the house of man." During Korean War, at the request of Admiral Radford, Commander-in-Chief, Pacific Fleet, he resumes uniform to evaluate and make recommendations regarding Navy photography. Exhibi-

tions: "Photographs of Picasso by Mili and Capa"; "Newly Acquired Photographs by Stieglitz and Atget"; "All Color Photography"; "51 American Photographers"; "Lewis Carroll Photographs."

1951 Exhibitions: "Korea" (war photographs); "Abstraction in Photography"; "Twelve Photographers"; "Forgotten Photographers"; "Memorable *Life* Photographs" (wrote foreword and comment for book on show); "Photographs as Christmas Gifts"; "Five French Photographers: Brassaï, Cartier-Bresson, Doisneau, Ronis, Izis."

1952 January 15: Reviews and analyzes a showing of important abstract films in a lecture and presentation entitled "Why Experimental Films?" under the auspices of the Junior Council of The Museum of Modern Art. April: Receives *Popular Photography Magazine* Award "for his conspicuous influence on the progress of photography as an art, science and industry, through the inspiration and progressive leadership he has exercised over photography in America." Begins preparation of "The Family of Man" for The Museum of Modern Art, visiting 29 cities in 11 European countries in quest of photographs. Initiates a series of exhibitions entitled "Diogenes with a Camera." Edward Weston, Frederick Sommer, Harry Callahan, Esther Bubley, Eliot Porter, W. Eugene Smith in the first of these; II features Ansel Adams, Dorothea Lange, Tosh Matsumoto, Aaron Siskind, Todd Webb. Another show of the year: "Then (1839) and Now (1952)."

1953 Selects the American Section for "The Exhibition of Contemporary Photography—Japan and America" at The National Museum of Modern Art, Tokyo. Exhibitions: "Always the Young Strangers"; "Post-War European Photography."

1954 March 25: Dinner at The Museum of Modern Art to celebrate 75th birthday (March 27). Establishment of The Edward Steichen Purchase Fund announced by Museum.

1955 January 24: Opening of "The Family of Man" exhibition. Steichen receives the Newspaper Guild's "Front Page Award" for the Museum, and also awards from the American Society of Magazine Photographers, the Philadelphia Museum School of Art, the National Urban League, and Kappa Alpha Mu for this "Greatest of all photography exhibitions." Goes to Japan to arrange for the production there of "The Family of Man." Opens the exhibition in Berlin, as well as in Paris, and visits Amsterdam, Munich, and London to prepare for other showings. May 9: His photograph of the Rodin "Balzac" in the Museum's Sculpture Garden appears in *Life,* close to a half century after he made the Moonlight Series at Meudon. Growing preoccupation with "The Shad-blow Tree" on his Connecticut estate begins a five-year photographic dedication in color.

1956 Exhibitions: "Diogenes III: Manuel Alvarez Bravo, Walker Evans, August Sander, Paul Strand"; "Diogenes IV: Schenk, William Garnett, Marie-Jean Beraud-Villars, Shirley C. Burden"; "Contemporary American Photography" at the Musée d'Art Moderne in Paris; "Language of the Wall: Parisian Graffiti Photographed by Brassaï."

1957 February 19: Illustrated lecture, "Experimental Photography in Color," at The Museum of Modern Art. Death of Mrs. Steichen. June 21: Receives Honorary Doctorate of Fine Arts from the University of Wisconsin. Grows beard. Accepts first Annual Award "for outstanding achievement in fostering international understanding through photography" from Nippon Kogaku K.K.—an honor attained by vote of photographers, photographic organizations, and editors throughout the world, polled by the P.S.A. November 26: Exhibition "70 Photographers Look at New York" opens. Begins experimenting with painting again. Suffers stroke.

1958 Exhibition: "Photographs from the Museum Collection."

1959 Starts making motion picture film of "The Shad-blow Tree" in color. Receives Distinguished Service Award of the New York Botanical Society. March 27: Celebrates 80th birthday. Goes to Russia with Carl Sandburg for opening of "The Family of Man" in Moscow, where (as reported in *The New York Times* of September 5) a critique prepared under the supervision of the psychologist Ralph K. White of the U.S.I.A. gives the show "top rating in 'total impact'" in the American Exhibition. Also visits photographers in Stockholm, Paris, London. Becomes Chairman of the National Urban League project, "America's Many Faces." Exhibition: Photography Section of "Toward the New Museum of Modern Art." *Beethoven's Beloved* by Dana Steichen posthumously published. Suffers second stroke.

1960 Exhibitions: "The Sense of Abstraction"; "Toward the New Museum of Modern Art: Photography Section II"; photographs included in "Portraits from the Museum Collection"; "Photographs for Collectors" (for Museum's Art Lending Service); Section in museum-wide "Recent Acquisitions" exhibition. March 19: Marries Joanna Taub. June 5: Receives Honorary Doctorate of Fine Arts from the University of Hartford. Receives "German Prize for Cultural Achievement in Photography" from the Photographic Society of Germany. Suffers long illness. Starts to prepare for retrospective show.

1961 March 27: The exhibition "Steichen The Photographer" opens, in honor of his 82nd birthday. On this occasion, he receives the Premier Award of The Royal Photographic Society of Great Britain—the Silver Progress Medal for 1960—and in his honor the Photographic Society of Germany awards "The Edward Steichen Prize for Cultural Achievement in Photography" to August Sander. Announcement is made of plans for The Edward Steichen Photography Center in the new Museum of Modern Art to be. First foreigner to receive Award from the Photographic Society of Japan. Is the subject of a two-hour television program, "Heritage" (WQED—WQEX). Exhibition: "Diogenes with a Camera V" (Bill Brandt, Lucien Clergue, and Yasuhiro Ishimoto). September 26: Delivers Keynote Speech on "The Photographer and His Times" at the ASMP Asilomar Conference. November 16: Receives the 1961 ART IN AMERICA Award.

1962 Exhibition: Photographs by Harry Callahan and Robert Frank. February 15: Gives illustrated lecture at The Museum of Modern Art, on "Toward Abstraction." April 25: Placed on Honor Roll of the ASMP. May 26: Receives Honorary Degree from Lincoln College. July 1: Resignation as Director of The Department of Photography at The Museum of Modern Art becomes effective. Is given the title of Director Emeritus. October 15: Directs exhibition—"The Bitter Years: 1935–1941 Rural America as Seen by the Photographers of the Farm Security Administration"—at The Museum of Modern Art. Edits Museum publication on exhibition.

1963 July 4: Awarded Presidential Medal of Freedom by President John F. Kennedy.

1973 Dies March 25.

Picture Credits

(The numbers are the plate numbers, and the credits are to the owners of the prints. All prints reproduced in the book are bromide, unless otherwise noted.)

Albright-Knox Art Gallery, Buffalo, N.Y.: 59.

The Art Institute of Chicago, Chicago, Illinois, The Alfred Stieglitz Collection: 8, 13, 18, 42.

Collection of Mr. Shirley C. Burden, Beverly Hills, California: 210.

Collection of Mr. and Mrs. Hans Hammarskiöld, Stockholm, Sweden: 16.

Collection of Miss Grace M. Mayer, New York, N.Y.: 15.

The Metropolitan Museum of New York, N.Y., Gift of Alfred Stieglitz: 3, 12, 20, 23, 25, 28, 32, 34, 35, 36, 38, 40, 41, 43, 45, 46, 51, 52, 53, 57.

The Museum of Modern Art, New York, N.Y.: 1, 2, 4, 5, 6, 7, 9, 14, 17, 19, 22, 24, 26, 27, 29, 30, 31, 33, 37, 39, 44, 47, 48, 49, 50, 54, 55, 56, 58, 60, 61, 62, 63, 64, 65, 66, 67, 68, 69, 70, 71, 72, 73, 74, 75, 76, 77, 78, 79, 80, 81, 82, 83, 84, 85, 86, 87, 88, 89, 90, 91, 92, 93, 94, 95, 100, 101, 102, 103, 104, 105, 106, 107, 108, 109, 110, 111, 112, 113, 114, 115, 116, 117, 118, 119, 120, 121, 122, 123, 124, 125, 126, 127, 128, 129, 130, 131, 132, 133, 135, 136, 137, 138, 139, 140, 141, 142, 143, 144, 145, 146, 147, 148, 149, 150, 151, 152, 153, 154, 155, 156, 157, 158, 159, 160, 161, 162, 163, 164, 164a, 165, 166, 167, 168, 169, 170, 171, 172, 173, 174, 175, 176, 177, 178, 179, 180, 181, 182, 183, 184, 185, 186, 187, 188, 189, 190, 191, 192, 193, 194, 195, 196, 197, 198, 199, 200, 201, 202, 203, 204, 205, 206, 207, 208, 209, 211, 212, 213, 214, 215, 216, 217, 218, 219, 220, 221, 222, 223, 224, 225, 226, 227, 228, 229, 230, 238, 239, 240, 241, 242, 243, 244, 245, 246, 247, 248, 249.

The Philadelphia Museum of Art, Philadelphia, Pennsylvania: 21.

The Royal Photographic Society of Great Britain, London, England: 10, 11.

(The following pictures, whose ownership is credited above, were taken for the publications, agencies, and organizations indicated.)

For *Vanity Fair* (Photographs taken for *Vanity Fair* and *Vogue* appeared therein from 1923 to 1936 and were copyrighted by The Condé Nast Publications Inc.): 95, 115, 118, 119, 120, 122, 123, 124, 126, 127, 128, 129, 130, 133, 135, 136, 139, 141, 142, 145, 150, 151, 152, 153, 156, 165, 168, 171, 172, 173, 175, 180, 181, 182, 183, 185, 187, 189, 191, 192, 193, 194, 195, 197, 198, 199, 201, 202, 203, 204, 205, 206.

For *Vogue*: 100, 101, 102, 103, 104, 105, 106, 107, 108, 140, 154, 155, 190, 200.

For *Life*: 164a.

For *Camera Work*: 48, 55.

For *Everybody's Magazine*: 56, 57.

For *Art et Décoration*: 96, 97, 98, 99.

For Stehli Silks: 109, 110, 111, 112.

For the J. Walter Thompson Agency: The Andrew Jergens Company, 157; Manhattan Eye, Ear and Throat Hospital, 158; New York Post-Graduate Hospital, 159; Eastman Kodak Company "Snapshots," 160, 161; Travelers Aid Society, 162, 163; Federation of Jewish Philanthropies, 164.

For *The First Picture Book—Everyday Things for Babies* by Mary Steichen Martin, Harcourt, Brace and Company, 1930: 209.

For *Walden* by Henry David Thoreau, The Limited Editions Club, 1936: 215.

For the United States Navy: 223, 224, 225.